# Quarterly Essay

## CONTENTS

Quarterly Essay is published four times a year by Black Inc., an imprint of Schwartz Publishing Pty Ltd
Publisher: Morry Schwartz

ISBN 186 395 094X
ISSN 1832-0953

Subscriptions (4 issues): $49 a year within Australia incl. GST (Institutional subs. $59). Outside Australia $79. Payment may be made by Mastercard, Visa or Bankcard, or by cheque made out to Schwartz Publishing. Payment includes postage and handling.

To subscribe, fill out and post the subscription form on the last page of this essay, or subscribe online at:

www.quarterlyessay.com

Correspondence and subscriptions should be addressed to the Editor at:

Black Inc.
Level 5, 289 Flinders Lane
Melbourne VIC 3000 Australia
Phone: 61 3 9654 2000
Fax: 61 3 9654 2290
Email: quarterlyessay@blackincbooks.com
http://www.quarterlyessay.com

Editor: Chris Feik
Management: Sophy Williams
Production Co-ordinator: Caitlin Yates
Publicity: Meredith Kelly
Design: Guy Mirabella

## INTRODUCTION

How are we to understand the contribution of John Howard himself to the success of his governments? The question invites biographical speculation about Howard's personality, his family background, his early political career, his political skills and beliefs, as well as consideration of other possible contributing factors such as luck and the failings of Labor. This essay takes one tack through the many possible lines of enquiry about the reasons for Howard's phenomenal political success and argues that much of it can be explained by the skill with which he has drawn on the Liberal Party's traditions and rhetoric. To some extent it is a calming operation, using history to give a long view on the partisan struggles and passions of the present. Today Howard seems invincible, presiding over Australian politics like the veritable colossus and making it hard to think beyond and around him, especially for his opponents both inside and outside the Liberal Party.

To my mind much that has been written about Howard and his governments has been wrong, or at least overheated, particularly the claims about what his election victories show about the Australian people – that they are racist, uncaring, reactionary, and so on. Also overheated are many of the claims made about Howard himself. Hating a straw man may be emotionally satisfying, but it is not good politics. Making Howard out to be more radical or more cunning or more powerful than he is might explain to his opponents their own sense of futility, but it does nothing to connect with his arguments or his supporters.

Contemporary accounts caught up in the urgent conflicts of the day are probably always overheated. And a media forever scanning for the contours of the new is not good at noticing things that don't change. Of course, not all that's been written about the Howard governments is wrong, and I won't discuss all aspects of Howard's record in what follows. What I will do is look at how Howard has played the politics of the nation, and argue that this has its origins in his party's history. I hope this will contribute to a more rounded understanding both of Howard and of the Liberal Party.

I do not particularly like the Howard governments, but nor am I wholly appalled by them. They have done some things I think are unforgivable, particularly in the area of indigenous affairs. Their record of cruelty is greater than previous governments, and they have corrupted practices of accountable government. They have been good at managing the finances of the budget, but poor long-term economic managers, and have wasted opportunities for reform. But they have not ended the world as we know it. And I'm not yet sure that they have fundamentally changed Australia.

When I look at Howard the continuities seem stronger than the ruptures. This may of course be a matter of temperament, of seeing the glass half full rather than half empty, but it is also about perspective. I write this essay not as a moralist but as a political historian. Nevertheless I am very aware of writing into a debate that is bitter and divided, where people who criticise the government are accused of being Howard-haters, and those who defend it of being apologists; where many politically engaged people feel angry and locked out; where neither side is really very interested in seeing the rationality of the other's position.

For me, a central task of political history is to inhabit political positions and explain them from the inside. This means taking seriously what people say about what they believe, and thinking hard about how and why they see the world as they do. This requires knowing the historical context: what is going on in the world people are forming their beliefs about. Political beliefs are partial representations of reality, and historians need to understand as much as they can about that reality if they are to perceive the patterns of partiality with which it is apprehended. But they also have to listen carefully to what people say they believe and not be too quick to dismiss them as opportunists, hypocrites or liars.

Judith Brett

# RELAXED AND COMFORTABLE | The Liberal Party's Australia

Judith Brett

## NATION

> We represent all the people, not just the ones who voted for us, but the ones who voted against us. And the real thing we have to produce is not only national prosperity but national unity.

With these words Robert Menzies accepted the responsibility of victory at the 1949 election, for the Liberal Party of Australia and its coalition partner, the Country Party. On the Movietone news footage his hair is already white, his heavy black eyebrows and jowls unmistakable. By the time he retires from office in early 1966 he will be seventy-two, the grand old man of the Liberals who delivered his party its longest run of political success.

For the major parties electoral politics is about the tension between unity and division. To put itself forward to govern the country, a party must be a plausible representative of the country as a whole. Yet in the adversarial politics of our system of parliamentary government, it must also compete, and present itself strongly as a representative of some interests and values and not others. It must rally its supporters and attack its opponents, and so speak the angry, self-righteous language of division as well as the reassurances of unity. Thus, at the end of the election, when the battle's been won, the party leader who is to become prime minister will reassure the nation that he will govern on behalf of them all, not just those who voted for him. This is an election-night ritual, but it can be more or less convincingly done. Menzies did it seven more times before he retired. In 1963, after his last election, he delivered the same message on television, thanking the ladies and gentlemen for the victory and again promising to govern for all. Menzies delivered the message seated alone at a desk, looking straight down the camera into the Saturday-night lounge rooms of the nation. There was none of the triumphalist hullabaloo of the election-night victory party to remind that this was all about winning and losing; there were no journalists present to ask awkward questions; there was no flicking of the eyes from the camera to the party faithful and back again. His voice was calm, intimate and reassuring, and he spoke only to you.

When Menzies led the Coalition to victory in December 1949, the Liberal Party of Australia was just short of five years old. It had been formed officially in early 1945, although the crucial decisions were made in the previous year. The Australian Labor Party, first under John Curtin and then under Ben Chifley, had led Australia through the war after taking office in 1941. It was a popular and effective wartime government, but made some bad mistakes afterwards. When Labor lost, no one, and certainly not those in the Liberal Party, foresaw the length of time it would spend in opposition.

At its foundation, the Liberal Party did not represent a new political force. It was not like the Greens, or the Labor Party in its early days, bringing new ideas and new social identities into the parliament. Rather, it was a new organisational form for ideas and political identities that had been central to Australian politics since Federation. The first Liberal Party emerged from Fusion in 1909 when Alfred Deakin's Victorian Liberals joined with George Reid's New South Wales free traders turned conservatives to present a united front against the newly powerful Labor Party. The 1910 election, which Labor won, consolidated the basic shape of the Australian party system, which still holds today.

In 1916, when Labor split over conscription, Prime Minister Billy Hughes and other pro-conscriptionists left to form a Nationalist government. A Nationalist Party quickly followed, which governed throughout the 1920s. When Labor split again in the Depression over how to manage the nation's finances, Treasurer Joseph Lyons led a small band across the party divide and the Nationalists re-formed to accommodate them. Honest Joe Lyons became the leader of the United Australia Party and soon after Prime Minister of Australia. The United Australia Party governed until 1941, when it was defeated on the floor of parliament and John Curtin was asked to form a government.

At the first two re-formations, names were chosen (Nationalists, United Australia Party) which put the new party forward as representing the nation as a whole and the presence of some ex-Labor men gave this claim temporary plausibility. The catalyst for the 1945 re-formation was different. By the early 1940s the United Australia Party was a discredited shambles and new parties were proliferating to compete for the non-labour vote. At the 1943 election the UAP received only 16 per cent of the vote. Menzies argued that the new party needed a name that was distinctive, that would show that it stood for something, in the same way that Labor's values showed in its name.

> We took the name Liberal because we were determined to be a progressive party ... in no sense reactionary, but believing in the individual, his rights, and his enterprise, and rejecting the Socialist panacea.

Non-labour's many names has always made writing non-labour's history difficult. Narratives have to be interrupted to explain an organisational change, and the rhetoric of new beginnings has obscured continuities. In particular the new beginning of the Liberal Party in 1945 has discouraged larger histories. Because the United Australia Party was discredited, the Liberal Party was keen to establish its distance from it. There were marked differences between the new and the old parties, particularly in organisation, but there was also a great deal of continuity. Core arguments and political values were continuous, as were the groups the parties looked to for electoral support. Historians have often used the term "non-labour" to describe this continuous political tradition, but it is a negative name, and can lead to thinking that this tradition is primarily negative and oppositional, playing the role, as Menzies described it, of "the man who says 'No'" in an Australian politics led by Labor. When I wrote a history of the major non-labour parties in twentieth-century Australia, I decided to call their supporters Liberals, as this was the name they had most often called themselves.

The new Liberal Party proved to be successful beyond its founders' wildest expectations. This year it celebrated its sixtieth anniversary. The party has led the government of Australia for forty of the fifty-five years since 1949. As I write this, John Howard is in his fourth term as prime minister. For Liberals, and for Howard himself, Menzies is the benchmark, and Howard is now second only to him in his electoral success and political dominance. He is, it might be said, on the way to becoming our Robert Menzies. But this would be a deceptive conclusion if it were taken to mean simply that Howard is repeating the ideas of Menzies. Rather, he is like Menzies in his mastery of the political tradition of Australian liberalism, and in his ability to adapt that tradition to present circumstances. The success of the Howard governments is neither aberration nor revolution. It is based in the twentieth-century history of the Liberal Party and its ability to present itself as the natural party of government.

## Origins

What then is the political tradition that the Liberal Party carries? It is the belief that it is the proper representative and guardian of the nation's interest. Here is Alfred Deakin, launching the first Commonwealth Liberal Party in the Melbourne Town Hall in 1909:

> This is not a policy aimed at the interests of any class. It is a national policy addressing itself in a practical manner to the practical needs of the people of Australia today.

And here is John Howard almost ninety years later in his 1996 Menzies Lecture:

> The Liberal Party has never been a party of privilege or sectional interests or narrow prejudice ... Liberalism has focused on national interests rather than sectional interests.

David Kemp, adviser to Malcolm Fraser and minister in Howard's governments, elaborated in a piece written after the Liberals lost the 1993 election:

> The Liberal Party's strength has always been the fact that it is not the voice of any narrow vested interests but a party genuinely of individual people, of the unorganised majorities. It can only be effective when it expresses their concerns and their values. These embrace the nature of Australian society and its history. They embrace such issues as the unity and constitutional stability of the country, which are now under threat.

Kemp refers here to Labor's moves to change the flag and make Australia a republic, two issues, he says, which will "divide generations of Australians from each other in a way that will take decades to repair".

The party of the class, the section, the part, the party that introduces conflict and division into the heart of the nation, is of course the Australian Labor Party. Labor is the Liberals' fundamental opponent, and it is not possible to understand the Liberals without also understanding something of the history of Labor. The Liberal and Labor parties are like two boxers in a never-ending fight; the feints and blows of one only make sense if we also know where the other is aiming and which are the hits that land, even if at times one boxer pretends he has the show all to himself. In an interview for a Sunday paper, Victorian Liberal leader Robert Doyle said that he was reading my book *Australian Liberals and the Moral Middle Class* with "great anger". "I find it astonishing", he said, "that this historian wanted to write a book about the Liberals and in paragraph two mentions the ALP." But it can't be otherwise. The first Liberal Party came into being as a direct consequence of the actions of Labor, and they have faced each other across the parliament and the electorate ever since.

In nineteenth-century Australia, political action centred on the colonial parliaments, which were composed of members who prided themselves on their independence and who came together in loose alliances to support or oppose the legislative program of the big men who dominated the chamber. It was common for governments to be defeated in parliament, and for parliamentarians to change allegiance, perhaps for the offer of a ministry or the promise of a railway through their electorate. At election time, leagues of citizens formed to canvass support for the various candidates. Between elections these leagues were all but moribund. There was nothing comparable to today's continuing party organisation, and the candidates were as likely to stress their independence as their membership of any particular political grouping. The independent MP was considered to be in a better position to strike a hard bargain for his vote in the chamber and so win resources for development projects in his electorate.

Vestiges of this history are still found in the Liberal Party's organisation today, in particular in the power of the parliamentary leader over party policy, and in the criticisms the Liberals make of the party organisation of their rival. In contrast to Labor, where policy is made by the state and federal conferences (in theory at least), the Liberal Party councils have the power only to advise. Also in contrast to Labor, there is no formal pledge to bind Liberal parliamentarians to the party platform. Labor is seen as the party of the machine, controlled by extra-parliamentary forces such as the union movement. When in the early 1960s Menzies attacked the ALP's federal executive as "36 Faceless Men", he was pointing out to the electorate that the Labor parliamentarians they voted for were not the ones making the party's policy. Rather it was being made by men outside the parliament, whom they had never voted for, and whose names and faces they did not even know.

Labor's organisation is also the product of its history. Labor parties were formed outside the parliament, by a labour movement seeking to build a political wing as an alternative to industrial action after the failure of the great strikes of the 1890s. The dramatic electoral success of these parties fundamentally changed parliamentary politics in Australia. Although working men had been voting in Australia since about 1860, parliamentarians were usually drawn from the upper and middle classes. Candidates had independent means, or pursued careers such as journalism and the law which they could combine with the work of a parliamentarian. Some of these MPs, like Alfred Deakin, were sympathetic to the workers' lot and had introduced legislation to improve working conditions. But they were not workers.

Payment of members of parliament, which was introduced in the 1890s, made it possible for working-class men to enter parliament. And the appeal to the working class to vote Labor connected with newly formed social identities and understandings. The depression of the 1890s had killed the dream of Australia as the working-man's paradise. Horizons of opportunity closed in and working-class communities solidified in the inner cities of the colonial capitals, and in the mining towns. Labor parties mobilised the emerging sense of class consciousness, arguing that working men should stop voting for middle-class men, no matter how kindly they were and sympathetic to the lot of the worker. Instead they should vote for workers like themselves.

Labor's first electoral success was in New South Wales in 1891 when, with 21.8 per cent of the vote, it won 35 seats out of 140 and held the balance of power. But electoral success was one thing, translating it into parliamentary strength another. Balance of power politics requires rock-solid party unity. Their opponents forced a vote on the wedge issue of the day, free trade versus protection, and Labor's parliamentary unity collapsed. Supporters outside the parliament were appalled that Labor's parliamentary strength could collapse so quickly. The result was the development over the next decade of procedures to bind Labor's parliamentary representatives to the decisions of the party organisation outside parliament: the pledge, the policy-making power of conference, the power of caucus in a Labor government.

Although Labor played a negligible role in the debates about Federation and the formation of the federal constitution, it won 19.24 per cent of the vote at the first federal election. The third party, along with Edmund Barton and Alfred Deakin's Liberal protectionists and George Reid's free traders, its presence destabilised the parliament. The Liberal protectionists were the middle party, but Deakin knew that given the structure of the Westminster system three must eventually become two. "What kind of a game of cricket ... could they play if they had three elevens instead of two, with one side playing sometimes with one side, sometimes with the other, and sometimes for itself?" Deakin asked in 1904. "Someone must give way for the benefit of the State, and which was to give way was the delicate issue." Deakin of course hoped it would be Labor, accepting that its future lay in alliance with his Liberals. But Labor's electoral support grew at each subsequent election: 31 per cent in 1903, 37 per cent in 1906, and 50 per cent in the watershed election of 1910 when Labor became the first party since Federation to win government in its own right. It was not Labor that needed allies now, but Deakin's Liberals, and Deakin led his party to join with its erstwhile enemy and form a new, fused, non-labour party.

This was not what the Liberals, the free traders, or any of the other established colonial political groupings had envisaged when they welcomed in the new federation. They couldn't quite understand how it had happened, and they never quite accepted the legitimacy of Labor in parliament. At its crudest, the outrage at Labor's political power expressed itself in the politics of class prejudice and the belief that working-class men were not fit to govern. The first Labor MPs were mostly skilled tradesmen. Many were self-taught and well-read, autodidacts like Billy Hughes, who could match literary quotes with his better-schooled opponents. But they were unfamiliar with the arts of government, and suspect when it came to handling public finances. How could men who had never handled an amount of money bigger than their weekly wage – and this many gave to their wives – be expected to run the country's budget? At best they would be prone to extravagance, at worst corruption. The Liberal Party has always been quick to accuse Labor of corruption and rorts, as when it believed it could smell the stench of corruption rising from Paul Keating's piggery.

Along with their hostility to Labor's organisation, the Liberals had another objection to Labor in parliament, which is heard in the quotations above from Deakin and Howard. Because the Labor Party represents the interests of a class, or a section, it cannot govern on behalf of the nation as a whole. Labor brought the language of class and of class conflict into national parliaments hitherto understood as representative assemblies of citizens. Citizens were individuals. The legitimacy of the government rested on their consent, the strength of the nation depended on their virtues and their hard work. The parties that represented them ideally competed for government on the basis of differing visions of the national interest supported by appeal to principles and values. The non-labour parties, in their idealised imaginings of themselves, did not appeal to self-interest or sectional interest but rather attempted to develop policy for the nation as a whole, to put before the citizens at election time for their verdict.

The objection to Labor as the party of class and section has proved more durable and flexible than the objection based on Labor's machine-like organisation, particularly as the Liberal Party has tightened party discipline over its parliamentarians on the one hand, and Labor's parliamentary leadership has asserted its independence from the party organisation on the other. Nevertheless the two criticisms are related. To the Liberals, it is because Labor parliamentarians are bound to Labor's party organisation and through it to the union movement that they are unable to act in the parliament as parliamentarians should, according to their view of the national interest.

It was over just such tensions between individual MPs' beliefs about the national interest and the policy of their party that Labor split: first in World War I when Labor parliamentarians who supported conscription defied the Labor Party's opposition to it; and again in 1931 when Joseph Lyons believed that his party's financial policies were damaging Australia's reputation for sound and honest financial practices. Labor, he said, required him to put the party before the nation, and this he could not and would not do. In both cases leading Labor men threw their lot in with the party that talked the language of the nation. They left the party of class, and appealed to the citizens of Australia on the basis of what they thought was right. Labor regarded them as rats. To the Liberals they were patriots and outstanding citizens.

Since 1910, although the Liberals have had no choice but to accept the bi-polar division of Australian politics, they have continued to refuse Labor's picture of Australia as divided between two conflicting classes or irreconcilable interests – bosses and workers, working class and middle class, capital and labour. They have consistently opposed Labor's language of class interest and class conflict by appealing instead to citizens' commitment to the nation as a whole and to their interests as free, unaffiliated, non-unionised individuals. After it became clear that the majority of those in the working class were responding to Labor, the Liberals became the party of the unorganised rest, the "residuum" as Frederic Eggleston described it – those people left over after Labor had captured the workers.

Australian Liberals thus developed a dual identity. Labor's political mobilisation of the working class forced the middle class to recognise itself as having distinctive, separate interests. At the same time Liberals deeply resented being forced into such a recognition, and refused to accept its legitimacy as a mode of understanding the polity or of developing policy for the nation. This resentfully accepted dual identity can be heard in the opening of Robert Menzies' famous 1942 radio broadcast to "The Forgotten People", which talks the language of class even as it denies its relevance.

## Class and the Forgotten People

> In a country like Australia, the class war must always be a false war. But if we are to talk of classes, then the time has come to say something about the forgotten class – The Middle Class – those people who are constantly in danger of being ground between the upper and nether millstones of the false class war; the middle class who, properly regarded, represent the backbone of this country.
>
> We don't have classes here as in England. It is necessary, therefore, that I should define what I mean when I use the expression "the middle class".

"We don't have classes here as in England." This is a central belief of Australian Liberals. The Old World might still have aristocrats and prejudiced snobs and people trapped in grinding deferential poverty, but the new world of Australia offers everyone a chance to participate in the shared task of nation-building and to enjoy its rewards. This is one half of the dual identity. With his other eye, Menzies sees the contours of a class-divided society, and he goes on in his speech to set out a three-part schema. At the top are the rich and powerful who are well able to look after themselves; at the "other end of the scale" are "the mass of unskilled people, almost invariably well-organised, with their wages and conditions safeguarded by popular law". The people in the middle are what's left, "the residuum". Menzies lists them: "salary earners, shopkeepers, skilled artisans, professional men and women, farmers and so on". Today we would describe them as small-business people and the self-employed. But what's crucial for Menzies' middle class is not who is included but why.

Membership is not based on a person's economic role, as in Labor's class-based schema. Rather it is based on virtue, strength of character, respectability and sense of responsibility. These are qualities possessed by individual people, and anyone may possess them, no matter what their job or their level of material wealth. Membership of the middle class is thus open to anyone who identifies with its virtues. A system of social classification of this kind, which is based on people's individual moral qualities, has wide commonsense appeal. It accords with Australians' egalitarian manners, in which we treat people on their merits. Here is Menzies reflecting at the end of his life on his own class origins:

> If social classes are, as they sometime are, based on money, then I was in the lowest stratum in Ballarat as a boy; but if classes depend on something else, some personal quality, then people like myself and my parents did not feel they were in any way out of it.

In fact they thought they were central, part of the backbone of the nation.

The image of the "backbone of the nation" is worth reflecting on, as it is used frequently by Liberals in the first three-quarters of the twentieth century. It is an organic image, with the nation conceived as a body, and so it contrasts implicitly with the more abstract conception of the nation divided into classes. The backbone holds the body together and gives it structure, just as the middle class is thought to do. Backbone is also a metaphor for independence and individual strength of character. People with backbone "do not want to live spineless and effortless on an all-powerful state"; they want to stand on their own two feet.

Self-evidently to the Liberals, the people with backbone are the backbone of the nation. Liberal individualism was in part a belief that the strength of the nation was based on the qualities of the individuals who composed it. As John Stuart Mill explained in *Considerations on Representative Government*:

> If we ask ourselves on what causes and conditions good govern-
> ment in all its senses, from the humblest to the most exalted,
> depends, we find that the principal of them, the one which tran-
> scends all others, is the qualities of the human beings composing
> the society over which the government is exercised.

From this perspective, it is not large historical forces that shape the national destiny, but rather the actions of individual men and women. And, of course, it is from individual men and women that politicians in a democracy must garner support.

Menzies' speech to the Forgotten People was one of a series of radio broadcasts he made on the Macquarie Network during 1942 and 1943 at 9.15 on a Friday night. This particular broadcast was made on 22 May and followed a program of plantation melodies – easy-listening music for the end of the working week and a diversion from the anxieties of war. Singapore had fallen in February, and Australia was on a total war foot-ing. Menzies was by this time already a consummate political communi-cator, master of all the theatres of politics: the cut and thrust of the hustings where he sharpened his wit on the hecklers; the closely argued parliamentary speech and the swift responses of Question Time; the well-fed joviality of the after-dinner speech. Franklin Roosevelt had been the first leader to show how politicians could use radio. In his fireside chats to Depression America he established a more direct and intimate connection with voters than was possible in the public rallies and meet-ings which had been the mainstay of electioneering until then. In the middle of the greatest collective effort Australians had ever engaged in, the wartime mobilisation in the face of the threat of Japanese invasion, Menzies appealed to people's private hopes for their lives after the war, and reminded them of the virtues and attitudes they bore as individuals. He singled them out from the mass, the crowd, the workplace, drawing them away from their class allegiances, talking to them in the place where they felt most themselves, the kitchens and lounge rooms of their homes.

The value of the middle class, Menzies told his listeners, was that it had a "stake in the country" though its "responsibility for homes – homes material, homes human and homes spiritual". He associated "homes material" with frugality and patriotism, "homes human" with ambition for one's children, and "homes spiritual" with commitment to independence and respect for liberal education and cultural achievement.

> I do not believe that the real life of the nation is to be found in great luxury hotels and the petty gossip of so-called fashionable suburbs, or in the officialdom of organised masses.
>
> It is to be found in the homes of people who are nameless and unadvertised, and who, whatever their religious conviction or dogma, see in their children their greatest contribution to the human race. The home is the foundation of sanity and sobriety; it is the indispensable condition of continuity; its health determines the health of society as a whole.

In the first paragraph, Menzies begins to locate the classes he has already defined in their characteristic dwelling places. The rich are in the hotels with their suggestion of sexual licence, or gossiping in their fashionable suburbs; the middle class are in the cosy homes they've worked so hard for; but where are the workers? One might expect them to be in rented rooms or over-crowded slums, but this of course would raise questions about distribution of wealth and the scarcity of housing, which was acute in the 1940s. The series slips a cog, and instead of working-class domestic space we encounter "the officialdom of organised masses". It is as if the members of the working class do not have homes and children, or rather that, insofar as they do, they are invited to identify themselves as middle class. The apparent lapse in logic reveals the deeper logic of the opposition Menzies is working with, which counterposes two ways of understanding society. Is society composed of individuals with varying moral and personal qualities, or of classes based on the impersonal forces of the economy? The home is where people are most likely to feel in control of their destiny, able to let down their guard and be relaxed and comfortable. Talking to people in their homes, Menzies was inviting listeners to identify their political interests not with their economic role and the conflicts of the workplace, which was Labor's turf, but with their private and domestic selves, and their private pleasures and ambitions. In doing so he was constructing the Liberals as the party able to govern for everyone.

## The Long Boom

History was kind to Menzies and the Liberals. The post-war boom brought undreamed-of affluence to Australia, and after winning the 1949 election the Liberal Party began to reap the electoral rewards. Historian John Murphy has argued persuasively that Australia experienced two 1950s. The first, lasting until about 1955, was filled with dread of an impending third world war fought with the new atomic weapons, and anxiety about a repetition of the economic instability and hardship that had followed World War I. In the second, after 1955, Australians began to relax and enjoy their prosperity and the security of full employment. Home ownership rates soared, from 53 per cent in 1947 to 63 per cent by 1954 and 70 per cent in 1961. The dream of the working-man's paradise that had been on hold since the depression of the 1890s was now being realised. By 1968, 94 per cent of the houses in Melbourne's working-class suburb of Clayton were owner-occupied.

Left interpretations of the political meaning of the post-war housing boom, and of the 1950s more generally, have seen this period as one of retreat from the public world and the obligations of citizenship. But this interpretation misses the link between home ownership, character, citizenship and nation which had long been self-evident to Australian Liberals. Liberal conceptions of citizenship bridged the gulf between public and private by asserting the relevance of domestic virtues to the public sphere. To build a home was to build a stake in the nation, a secure place to raise future citizens with the independence of mind and the strength of character on which the nation depended. Liberals had always dreamed that such secure bases would be available to everyone, and in the 1950s, to their surprise and everyone else's, they were.

History was also kind to the Liberals in another way: after the death of Ben Chifley, Labor was riven by conflict over communism. The party split of 1955, the subsequent formation of the DLP and the erratic and increasingly paranoid leadership of Bert Evatt all weakened Labor as an effective opposition and a plausible alternative government. Addressing the voters in 1955, Menzies could say, "The Labor Party, I regret to say, is not fit to govern. It can't rule itself, it's disunited … And you know in your hearts that that's true. And if you know that in your hearts, then on Saturday you'll know what to do." After Menzies retired, however, history got away from the Liberals as they struggled to govern a country increasingly divided over the Vietnam War. And the Labor Party began to rebuild. The crucial years were from 1966 to 1972. The Vietnam debate blew away the calm and settled positions of Australian politics that seemed, in the early 1960s, as if they would never change. In *The Lucky Country* Donald Horne summed up just how unrepresentative Menzies had become:

> It was a feature of Menzies' long rule that little of what he did seems to matter much … The positive characteristics of his Age – the spread of affluence, the considerable relaxation in social styles, the increase in national self-assurance, the continued migration programme, the beginning of an interest in Asia and the growing tolerance of Asians resident in Australia, the demands of technology, the increasing power of overseas investment in Australia – were not of the kind of thing that Menzies has "stood for" and some of them are the opposite of what he had hoped when he came to power.

When Menzies retired, the Liberal Party began to explore new, reforming policies. Harold Holt, famously photographed with his bikini-clad step-daughters-in-law, signalled the generational shift. Australia's racially restrictive immigration laws were all but dismantled, the referendum to give the Commonwealth power over Aboriginal affairs was initiated and won, and Australia's relations with Asia began to be re-thought.

Holt was succeeded by John Gorton, who continued the direction of Holt's reforms. He expanded the Commonwealth's support for the arts, made the first moves in the decolonisation of PNG, and began to involve the Commonwealth in managing the environment. Always a compromise candidate, however, he had insufficient political support or skill to survive for long as conflict mounted over Vietnam. He was succeeded by William McMahon, who was probably Australia's most inept past prime minister. He had even less chance of steering a nervous and fractious party through the reform process. The reforms undertaken by the Liberal governments in the seven years between the retirement of Menzies and the election of Whitlam in 1972 were substantial, but they have received little credit for them. Instead the credit went to Whitlam and Labor.

Gough Whitlam, a middle-class lawyer attracted to the ALP as the party of reform, set about developing comprehensive new policies to stake Labor's claim to government. These centred on health, social welfare, urban and regional planning and foreign policy, and on creative ways to circumvent the states. But the real long-term meaning of this period was being made on the streets and in the hearts and minds of the young, first in the anti-war movement and then in what became known as the new social movements.

This was a different sort of politics, happening outside the established institutions of parties, trade unions and pressure groups. It brought issues hitherto regarded as part of the private realm into the public domain of politics. Sexual liberation challenged heterosexual norms, while women's lib challenged patriarchal domination. Aboriginal activists, inspired by the US civil rights movement, challenged the racism of white Australia, and a radical environmental movement challenged the pressure-group politics of the older conservationists. New organisations formed and many people were swept up by a sense that the world – and their lives – could be different.

In its early days the labour movement had been a social movement, but it had long since settled into the groove of institutional politics with its elaborate party organisation and complex trade union politics. For their part the Liberals continued to present themselves as the responsible party of government. Both parties, though, had points of potential sympathetic connection with the new movements, based on their respective political traditions and values, as well as points of obvious disagreement.

Australian party conflict in the last thirty years has been fundamentally shaped by the relative fortunes of the Labor and Liberal parties when these new issues first reached the political agenda. It seems to me that it is not obvious, except in hindsight, that the new social movements should have attached themselves to the Labor Party. A Liberal Party led by Don Chipp would have offered them a congenial home. Drawing on traditional liberal thinking, it could have linked a longstanding commitment to economic rights and freedoms with the new civil rights being demanded. Barriers to people enjoying full equality of opportunity to develop their talents and capacities could have been recognised and remedied under a Liberal banner. This did not happen, and at this point the term small "l" liberal entered the Australian political lexicon, to distinguish political positions based on the classic nineteenth-century liberal arguments about the limits of the state's power over private behaviour from the more morally and socially conservative positions of the Liberal Party platform.

Pursuing the same line of counterfactual historical speculation, one could anticipate that a Labor Party led by a conservative, working-class Catholic like Arthur Calwell would have been an inhospitable place for men and women arguing for new sexual freedoms, or even for expanded opportunities for women; and had Labor not split in the 1950s there would have been many more Catholic men like Calwell in the party.

But there were also points of connection in Labor's traditions which shone the more brightly in a revitalised Labor Party filling with young political activists. Like earlier working-class politics, the new social movements focused attention on the circumstances that limit people's lives and they demanded that the state act to reform these. The new movements attached themselves to an ascending Labor Party as the party of hope and reform, and their causes were carried onto the national agenda by the momentum of Whitlam's win. Sexuality, gender, race and ethnicity joined class as potential sources of inequality and oppression. And the Liberals were forced back into the position of the man who says No.

After Fraser defeated the Whitlam government, the Liberal Party moved to respond to the new social agenda, drawing belatedly on its traditions of commitment to tolerance, individual rights and equality of opportunity. Fraser gave multiculturalism substance, and continued the process of the recognition of land rights begun under Whitlam. He also responded generously to the refugee crisis at the end of the Vietnam War and so initiated the first large-scale Asian immigration to Australia. And he gave the new environmental movement one of its first big wins when he effectively blocked sand-mining on Fraser Island by refusing export licences.

Fraser received little recognition for this. The emotions aroused by the dismissal of the Whitlam government made the opportunistic de facto marriage between Labor and the new social movements permanent. Fraser forfeited the trust of progressives with his determination to force the crisis that led to the Dismissal, and his confrontational anti-Labor rhetoric led many political activists and journalists to assume that he was driven by a doctrinaire commitment to undo everything associated with the Whitlam years. He never managed to convince them otherwise, and the new social issues – among them multiculturalism, feminism, environmentalism and a nascent reconciliation movement – were instead drawn into the Liberals' anti-Labor rhetoric of "special interests".

## In Opposition

After losing power in 1983, the Liberal Party went into a prolonged period of confusion, much as Labor is now experiencing. Divisions opened up over economic policy, with the so-called dries embracing the new economic rationalist agenda of reduced government spending and regulation, and gradually asserting their dominance over the wets who believed that government had a greater role to play. Because policy direction in the Liberal Party comes from the parliamentary party and the leader, these divisions were played out in a musical-chairs game of leadership changes, each one heralding a new beginning and each failing to bring either unity or electoral success to the party: Andrew Peacock, John Howard, Andrew Peacock, John Hewson and Alexander Downer. In 1995 Howard became leader again. Election victory has always been the main legitimator of Liberal leadership, and his defeat of Labor in 1996 stabilised his leadership.

Labor exploited their opponents' division, just as the Liberals are now doing to Labor. Leading Liberals generally agreed with the direction of Labor's economic reforms, except that they would move faster on labour market de-regulation. Labor's strategy, brilliantly executed by Keating in the 1993 election, was to push the Liberals as far to the right as possible and so make them carry all the anxiety about the economic reforms for which Labor was in fact responsible. It was also to push a progressive social agenda – to paint the Liberals as yesterday's men, still hankering after the Queen, the British Empire and white Australia.

The main game for Keating when he was treasurer was economic: de-regulating the economy to begin with, and then re-structuring it, diversifying the export base and reducing foreign debt. Once he became prime minister in 1991, he played for different stakes, and cultural and social issues moved to the centre of Labor's agenda. The three main items were reconciliation with indigenous Australians, embracing our geo-political position as part of Asia, and becoming a republic. These were presented forcefully, as the case for economic reform had been, and with fair doses of ridicule for those who opposed them. The republic in particular was a problem for the Liberals. Opinions were divided in the party and it was opposed by their coalition partner, the Nationals. But being prime minister is different from being treasurer, and arguing for change is harder. One has to be able to speak on behalf of all the people, not just some of them, and when arguing for radical cultural change one has to reassure as well as convince. Keating was never able to do this, to rise above partisan division and become a statesman. He was energised by conflict and brilliant at marshalling his aggression. This was exciting if you agreed with him, but very unsettling if you didn't. Arguing passionately for reform, he could make people feel he had no respect for their views and experiences, and his verbal skill could leave them floundering to put their feelings into words. His aggression was building reservoirs of resentment.

In his second stint as Liberal leader, Howard became the champion of those who felt silenced by Keating's bullying, and by the bullying of those who shared Keating's agenda of cultural reform. Howard's own experience during his first term as leader had formed his views on this matter. A divisive debate about Australia's immigration policy had rumbled through the 1980s, triggered by the historian Geoffrey Blainey's comments that, given Australia's long history of restricted immigration, present rates of Asian immigration might threaten social cohesion. It erupted again in 1988 after the government-commissioned Fitzgerald Report found low levels of popular support for the current immigration program. In the subsequent public debate Howard was backed into a corner in which he refused to rule out the possibility of an Australian government imposing some form of racial restriction on immigration intake. Insisting all the while that he did not advocate this, he stubbornly stood his ground on a government's right to consider all the options, and in doing so prolonged the debate. Howard's stance was deeply damaging to his credibility as a leader, both among sections of the Liberal Party and among broad elite opinion, and it contributed to his replacement as Liberal leader by Peacock a year or so later. Howard drew the conclusion that under Labor it was impossible for some topics to be discussed openly, and in particular that it was impossible to raise any doubts in public about either immigration or multiculturalism without being accused of racism.

When Howard became leader again in 1995, Keating faced an opponent equally skilled in aggression, though less flashy, with far greater stamina, and more disciplined in selecting his targets. In my view Keating's prime ministership created the possibility for Howard's. In 1987, against the consensual leadership style of Hawke, Howard's conflictual politics had failed, but as prime minister Keating sharpened the lines of conflict. He marked out the territory, claiming Aboriginal reconciliation, multiculturalism and the republic for Labor, and so boxed the Liberals in and made a bipartisan approach to these issues difficult to achieve. All Howard then had to do was to reverse the meanings, and turn support for the values Keating was ridiculing into a winning rather than a losing strategy. Refusing the label of the man who said No to minorities, Howard became the man who said Yes to middle Australia.

What Howard did is what Liberals have always done. He made his stand firmly at the centre, and fought Labor from there, renewing the opposition between the Liberals' claim to the consensual centre and Labor as the party of the illegitimate section. Whatever it is called, the nation, the national interest, the Australian way of life, ordinary Australians, middle Australia, the mainstream, the broad cross-section, this is the political space which the Liberal Party claims as its own. From within it, Howard accused Labor of fomenting conflict and division in the heart of the nation, of dividing Australian from Australian, of ignoring the mainstream in favour of the noisy, self-interested few. A Liberal government would govern for all Australians, not just for some. Here is a long quote from a speech Howard made in June 1995 to the Menzies Research Centre:

There is a frustrated mainstream in Australia today which sees government decisions increasingly driven by the noisy, self-interested clamour of powerful vested interests with scant regard for the national interest ... Many Australians in the mainstream feel utterly powerless to compete with such groups, who seem to have the ear of government completely on major issues.

This bureaucracy of the new class is a world apart from the myriad of spontaneous, community-based organisations which have been part and parcel of the Australian mainstream for decades. Under us, the views of all particular interests will be assessed against the national interest and the sentiments of all Australians.

For the past twelve years Labor has governed essentially by proxy through interest groups. Identification with a powerful interest group has been seen as the vehicle through which government largesse is delivered.

Increasingly Australians have been exhorted to think of themselves as members of sub-groups. The focus so often has been on where we are different − not on what we have in common. In the process our sense of community has been severely damaged. Our goal will be to reverse this trend. Mainstream government means making decisions in the interests of the whole community, decisions which have the effect of uniting, not dividing the nation.

When I read this passage, more than anything else I hear its continuity with Liberal Party tradition. I hear the voice of Alfred Deakin arguing against sectional class-based interests, and I hear the voice of Robert Menzies reassuring the powerless and unorganised Forgotten People. Left commentators on Howard, including many political science academics, read the same speech and hear something quite different. They notice the reference to the bureaucracy and the new class and they hear the imported rhetoric of right-wing populism. They write essays which explain how Howard borrows his arguments about special interests and the power of the elites from right-wing American think-tanks and public choice theory, giving little or no consideration to the Australian sources of his ideas. Of course it is satisfying to belittle Howard as the mouthpiece of powerful foreign ideas, Gerry Gee on the knee of Reagan and Thatcher or George W. Bush and the neo-cons, but doing this only makes his political success harder to understand and so more infuriating for his opponents, driving them to search for explanations in the paranoid politics of outside influences or the pathology of the electorate.

If instead we see that Howard inherited the idea of a polity divided between, on the one hand, good representatives of the national interest and, on the other, bad vested interests pursuing their selfish designs with scant regard for the wellbeing of all, then we see that it is a simple matter for him to add a few more vested interests to the list, throwing the "elites" into the same camp as unions and the social movements. Nor is it then so puzzling that people respond to him. They are hearing arguments they have heard before; for some these are the same arguments that shaped their political identity, as they did for the young John Howard hearing how selfish unions made life difficult for hard-working small-business people like his father.

## A Nation of Individuals

There is, however, more to the Liberals' claim to the consensual centre than simply saying it's ours. The mainstream is conceived of in a particular way – as the space of unorganised, unaffiliated individuals formed into a community by their shared experience of and allegiance to the nation. Here is Howard again from the same 1995 speech:

> Central to my beliefs about the Australian character and the way in which Australia should be governed is the simple proposition that those things which unite us as Australians are infinitely greater and more enduring than the things which divide us.

Howard has well-developed ideas about the origins and virtues of the

Australian character. But before discussing these, more needs to be said about his understanding of unity and division in Australia. There is no better source for this than *Future Directions*, the policy document developed in Howard's first period as leader that provided the first detailed account of his thinking. It was a clumsy document with ponderous, impersonal prose, and the cover image of a blonde wife, a suited husband and two neat, clean children in front of a white picket fence was a cliché that invited ridicule. Nevertheless, its mixture of dry economics, social policies to support families, and an assimilationist nationalism, has been the basis on which Howard has built his electoral success.

*Future Directions* was launched to a theme song written by Bruce Courtney about a plain man, played to a country beat and with the repeated refrain, "Son, you're Australian, that's enough for anyone to be." What is most significant in this refrain is not the obvious appeal to nationalism but rather the dismissal of affiliations to social groups and identities larger than the family and smaller than the nation: to class, religion, ethnicity, region, gender, race. Thus, in a section called "Building One Australia", *Future Directions* rejects:

> so-called multicultural programmes which simply ensnare individuals in ethnic communities denying them the opportunity to fully participate in Australian society

and

> treaties with Aboriginal Australians which would permanently recognise them as citizens apart, unable to participate in the mainstream of Australian life, even where they wished to do so. Where communities are kept separate from Australian society there is no equality of opportunity.

Family and nation are enough for anyone. Other allegiances, other bases of social identity, risk limiting the freedom of the individual and dividing the nation. The part, the section, has returned in a new guise.

These passages show the underlying social imagination which Howard brought to the negotiation of claims by particular social groups when he won power in 1996. Those deep elements of identity politicised by the social movements – whether one is male or female, Aboriginal or settler Australian, Muslim or Christian, gay or straight – are understood as differences of individuals. The Liberals have been able to expand their concept of individual rights to include many of the policies of non-discrimination and equal opportunity demanded by the social movements, but arguments arise over how far these rights can be extended, and whether the recognition of the rights of some individuals compromises the rights of others. Has the expansion of opportunities for married women with children to work compromised the rights of women who choose to stay at home? Do all women have the right to state assistance with fertility treatment irrespective of their personal circumstances or sexual orientation? Might the rights of children be infringed by state policies which deny them real fathers? Should the state sanction committed non-heterosexual relationships by according them the status of marriage? It is not surprising that all these examples come from the sphere of family life. The family as an interdependent, mostly biologically based social unit resists dissolution into an association of rights-bearing individuals, in particular the relationship between parents and child. This marks the fault-line within contemporary politics between small "l" liberals and those who call themselves conservatives, and it runs through both the Labor and Liberal parties.

The most deeply unsettling of the new group-based demands arising in the 1970s were the claims of indigenous Australians. Leaving aside complex legal and political questions about indigenous sovereignty, the communal identities of indigenous Australians confront the Liberal social imagination with an intractable problem. Like the family, Aboriginal communities resist being dissolved into associations of rights- and duty-bearing individuals. Moral credibility is important to Liberals, yet in the area of indigenous policy they have been unable to formulate policies and positions morally acceptable to indigenous Australians (and to many nonindigenous Australians too). Much of the discussion of this failure has focused on race, but the difficulties go deeper than that.

In their own terms Australian Liberals are not racist, and to insist that they are simply reinforces their sense of misunderstood self-righteousness. Australian Liberals are modern individualists, and they see traditional societies based on ascribed identities and non-negotiable reciprocal obligations as trapping people, preventing them from participating in all that modern Australian life has to offer.

Australian Liberals understand racism as the belief that a racially defined group of people is inherently inferior and hence that it is legitimate for another group, which regards itself as inherently superior, to deny them equal rights. While they acknowledge that some people – including Liberals – have held such beliefs in the past, contemporary Liberals do not. Since the 1960s, they have accommodated the demand for non-racially discriminatory citizenship both for immigrants and for indigenous Australians. They have embraced the formal granting of *political* citizenship and acknowledged the legitimacy of the indigenous demand for equal *social* citizenship, and they recognise that the latter is still a long way from being achieved. In fact, Howard has moved the achievement of equal social rights, the overcoming of disadvantage, to the centre of the Liberals' indigenous policy. This position was already set out in *Future Directions*:

> As with other disadvantaged Australians what is needed is a sensitive commitment to eliminate those impediments which prevent Aborigines from enjoying the equality of opportunity to fulfil their own personal goals and choose their own life style that has been enjoyed by all Australians. (my italics)

The characteristic Howard most often attributes to indigenous Australians is disadvantage. This provides the justification for spending government money on targeted health, housing or employment programs at the same time as it makes clear that these programs are no different from those for any other disadvantaged Australians. Nor does Howard imagine that indigenous Australians would want to live any differently. Earlier this year he announced a review of Aboriginal communal land tenure established under the land rights legislation.

> I certainly believe that all Australians should be able to aspire to owning their own home and having their own business; having title to something is the key to your sense of individuality, it's the key to your capacity to achieve, and to care for your family and I don't believe that indigenous Australians should be treated differently in that respect.

From this perspective, there are only individual Australians, some of whom happen to be Aboriginal, and many of the most difficult political problems about the relations between Aboriginal and settler Australians simply disappear, as does the desire of Aboriginal groups to hold on to their traditional ways of life.

Since multiculturalism it has been easier to recognise that indigenous Australians have a distinctive cultural heritage, but it does not follow from this that they possess any distinctive rights or should receive any special treatment. Australian Liberals argue that indigenous Australians are members of the one Australian nation and should be treated the same as everyone else; to treat them differently would be to re-introduce racially based policies. On this basis John Howard has repeatedly opposed calls for a treaty with Aboriginal peoples. "It is an absurd proposition that a nation should make a treaty with its own citizens. It also denies that Aboriginal people have full citizenship rights now." A form of land title which can be enjoyed by only one group of Australians, recognition of customary law, talk of treaties and sovereignty – all these things offend against Australian Liberals' commonsense understanding of equality. They are seen as divisive, setting one group of Australians against another. The limits of Australian Liberalism are reached when claims are made which go beyond non-discrimination and equal citizenship to a recognition of indigenous rights.

The slogan for the 1996 election expressed Howard's core strategy of reclaiming the nation for the Liberals. If elected, the Liberal Party would govern "for all of us" – for all Australians, not just for some. The 1996 election was more a rejection of Keating and Labor than it was an embrace of Howard's vision and the Coalition's policies. Howard as leader presented a small target, with few policies and little detail. He campaigned on Labor's economic record of causing the recession we had to have at the end of the 1980s, and he promised a change in the national mood from the divisiveness and aggression which the Liberals claimed were characteristic of Keating's prime ministership.

Pamela Williams has written a fascinating book on the 1996 election campaign, charting the daily shifts in mood of the two campaign teams, the divisions over strategy, and the building momentum of Howard's win. It's full of detail for political junkies, but the big picture that comes through is the failure of Keating to project himself as a leader for the nation as a whole, to occupy the position of the statesman that was his for the taking as prime minister. To be able to lead your party into an election as the prime minister is a huge political asset, but Keating was psychologically and emotionally unable to take advantage of it. Instead he wanted a negative campaign, with blood in the water. Perhaps he thought he could do Howard slowly, as he had Hewson. But Howard was a far more experienced politician than Hewson. He was not easily thrown off message, and he could talk to the electorate. While Keating boasted of his foreign policy achievements in Asia, Howard talked about the problems facing families and small businesses; and he took the fight right up to Labor. "Don't any of you ever be lectured by the Labor Party about racial tolerance, never, ever."

The ABC made a matching pair of *Four Corners* programs on the two leaders. The title of the Keating program was "The Big Picture Man", the Howard one "An Average Australian Bloke". Even the articles tell a story here, Keating's definite "The" setting him apart from the crowd in a way eschewed by Howard's indefinite "A". The title of the program on Howard came from his answer to interviewer Liz Jackson when asked how he would describe himself. "I'm a quintessential Australian," he said, "an average Australian bloke." At the end of the program she asked him about his vision for Australia in the year 2000 and he replied, "An Australian nation that feels comfortable and relaxed about three things: about their history, about their present and the future."

As with Menzies' appeal to the Forgotten People, there was an edge of grievance to the slogan "For All of Us". The Liberal's campaign director, Andrew Robb, said the slogan "was aimed predominantly at middle Australia … to reach people who legitimately felt betrayed. What we were saying was that in governing, we would not just consider the wellbeing of a select few, but we would consider the broad national interest. We would govern not just for some, but for all of us." As Howard told the State Council of the Queensland Liberal Party, "Our slogan 'For All of Us' brought together in a very effective fashion the mood and the resentments of the Australian people towards the type of government that they had experienced over thirteen years."

The pitch was overwhelmingly successful. A Liberal exit poll identified a shift to the Coalition of a significant section of Labor's blue-collar male voter base. Andrew Robb gloated that this "significantly broadened the Coalition's voting base within middle Australia. And this movement overwhelmingly comes from workers and their families – Howard's battlers." The term was quickly taken up by journalists and pundits to explain the election results. Like Menzies' Forgotten People, Howard's battlers were unorganised individuals, their identity located in family and local community, their resources limited in comparison with those of their opponents – whether these be unionists, multiculturalists, republicans, feminists, environmentalists, the Aboriginal industry or the elites of the chardonnay set.

The Liberals' campaign slogan has provoked a great deal of discussion. Noel Pearson said that when he first heard "For All of Us", he thought "but not for them", and knew that indigenous Australians were being positioned as one of the noisy minorities. His foreboding was confirmed by Pauline Hanson's maiden speech in September 1996 in which she identified Aborigines as the main beneficiaries of government programs that look after minorities while ignoring the needs of ordinary people like herself. There was a stronger sense in the 1996 campaign of what the Liberal Party opposed than what it stood for, and during its first term in government many more grievances flooded into the consensual centre than Howard and the Liberals had bargained for, leaving them struggling to regain control of the political agenda from Hanson and her new One Nation Party.

Many left commentators have seen the slogan "For All of Us" as marking the beginning of a right populist turn in Australian politics. As I indicated at the outset of this essay, I am not so sure. I think its continuities with Liberal traditions are strong. Nevertheless there is something in the accusation. Pronouns matter in politics. "Uncle Sam needs you!" "We will never surrender." "I have spoken." "The government will be governing for you." "For all of us." Pronouns position speaker and audience; they gather some people together and exclude others; they elevate or disguise the self. Occasionally a pronoun slips through that makes us gasp, as when Philip Ruddock referred to a small boy going mad in detention as "it". When Menzies promised in 1963 to govern for all of you, the second person marked a stately, patrician distance between the responsibilities of government and the lives of the governed. And because it was ambiguous in its reference – singular or plural? – it did not so quickly conjure up a sense of collective identity and a "them" excluded from sharing that identity. The shift from "you" to "us" is thus significant. It evokes a stronger sense of collective identity, and it collapses the distance between government and governed.

## Howard's Australia

This is as Howard wanted it. Where Keating spoke to the nation, Howard spoke from it – straight from the heart of its shared beliefs and common-sense understandings of itself. This is revealed in the images which surround the two men. Keating's are of foreignness – his Italian suits, his love of German music and French clocks. Howard's are of suburban ordinariness – barbecues, cricket, the annual holiday at the same beachside resort, jogging in a shiny tracksuit festooned with logos. At stake here is not just what the two leaders think about Australia, but their different ideas about the proper role of government in relation to national experience. Keating, in keeping with the Labor Party's more reforming and interventionist tradition, believed that government has a responsibility to lead from out front. This might involve telling people they need to change, or legislating to force them to do so. Howard, with his Liberal commitment to smaller, less interventionist government, does not think it is the role of government to impose cultural change from above. The state may be the expression of the unity of the nation, but it is certainly not its creator. Rather that unity comes from the historical experiences and daily practices of the people. This is how Howard put it in his 1997 Australia Day speech:

> The symbols we hold dear as Australians and the beliefs that we have about what it is to be an Australian are not things that can ever be imposed from above by political leaders of any persuasion. They are not things that can be generated by [a] self-appointed cultural elite who seek to tell us what our identity ought to be. Rather they are feelings and attitudes that grow out of the spirit of the people.
>
> I've long held the belief that those things that we hold dear as Australians, those myths if you like, those legends about Australia, are those that essentially have come in two ways. They have come out of great traumatic events such as the events of the 25th of April 1915 in the Dardanelles on the beaches of Gallipoli and there are

those other things that through long usage and custom and a feeling that it suits the temperament of the Australian people we have come to love and hold dear. And I think of our tradition of informal mateship and egalitarianism. And I think it is very important when we think of our identity we remember that essentially it grows out of the spirit of the people and it is never something that can be imposed.

In reforming the culture Howard believes that governments can only move as fast as the people want them to. Notice that Howard is talking specifically here about national identity, not about a government's responsibilities across the board. He has not been a slavish follower of public opinion when it comes to economic reform, as evidenced by his dogged support of unpopular economic policies like the GST and the full privatisation of Telstra; nor in foreign policy, where he took Australia into the "coalition of the willing" with the United States against the anti-war mood registered in the opinion polls. In both cases, gambling that the advantages of incumbency would turn the tide of popular opinion his way, he has drawn on the Liberal Party's traditions of providing what they see as good government in the national interest. But when arguing against Keating's cultural agenda, he draws on a different strand in his party's traditions – the one I have been elaborating here – which claims that the Liberal Party is the party best able to understand and represent the nation.

As prime minister, Howard has found many occasions to speak to Australians about themselves and to fill out what he means by "the temperament of the Australian people": addresses on Australia Days and Anzac Days, eulogies on the deaths of famous Australians like Don Bradman and Gallipoli veteran Alec Campbell, countless speeches to community organisations, and at state occasions such as the celebrations to mark the 2001 Centenary of Federation. Here are some examples:

Our society is underpinned by those uniquely Australian concepts of a fair go and practical mateship.

Being Australian means doing the decent thing in a pragmatic and respectable society which lives up to its creed of practical mateship … Australians are a down-to-earth people. It is part of our virtue. Rooted deep in our psyche is a sense of fair play and a strong egalitarian streak.

Being Australian embodies real notions of decency and pragmatism in a classless society which lives up to its creed of practical mateship.

The openness and unpretentious character of Australians has given us a well-deserved reputation for tolerance and hospitality.

When the self-esteem of a generation of young men was under challenge [in the Depression], the feats of Bradman reminded them that Australians were capable of being a competitive talented and resourceful people. His success also reinforced the national spirit, which was born out of the Australian sacrifice during World War I and helped to display the independence and self-reliance of a young nation barely decades old.

In our highest aspirations I imagine that Weary Dunlop represents what so many of us would like to be as Australians. He had that uncomplicated generosity and decency. He had enormous strength as well as those laconic characteristics which we hold so dear as being part of the Australian existence and Australian personality.

In only a few short weeks Australia will celebrate a centenary of nationhood. A century during which only four generations fashioned a unique culture, created a decent, tolerant and cohesive society, built a thriving modern economy, nurtured some of the finest democratic traditions ever practised and earned gratitude and respect from nations around the world.

Howard is not a great rhetorician, and his statements of the nation's virtues are not particularly memorable. They do, however, articulate ideas about what it is to be Australian with deep roots in both historical and contemporary experience. In the middle 1950s the radical historian Russel Ward published a book called *The Australian Legend*, in which he described a set of distinctive Australian character traits forged from the nineteenth-century settlers' experience of the land: egalitarianism, practical improvisation, scepticism towards authority, larrikinism, loyalty to mates, informality, generosity. Ward claimed that the Australian tradition was inherently radical and that ordinary Australians were naturally left-wing. The itinerant rural labourers who formed the first labour parties bore its virtues, as did the Australian diggers of World War I, and it captured aspects of Australian working-class culture and its collectivist political traditions. Until Howard, the Labor Party was more comfortable with the language of mates and the fair go than the Liberals, who instead spoke a language of respectability and support for the institutions of the state. As well, the Australian Legend can be uncompromisingly masculinist, and valorise irresponsible, larrikin masculinity – the wild colonial boy – at the expense of the settled commitment of suburban home-makers to whom the Liberals have always pitched their appeal. But the character traits of the Australian Legend were always more politically protean than Ward or Labor recognised. Conservative country people have their own version in the Pioneer Legend, and easygoing, co-operative informality is as likely to be found in suburban sports clubs as in trade unions.

What about the present? A recent focus-group study found broad agreement with the Legend's characterisation of the typically Australian values and character traits. The groups interviewed for the study were diverse across class, gender and place of residence, and included one group of non-English-speaking women. Participants were asked to identify Australian individuals, clubs and organisations, activities and events, and values and beliefs, and to explain the reasons for their choices. The researchers found remarkable agreement across the groups. Moreover, different "Australian" things were tied together by chains of mutually supporting symbolic association. Explaining why a particular person epitomises Australia, the respondents drew on values and beliefs which they subsequently characterised as Australian, or cited their membership of Australian organisations such as voluntary fire brigades or surf life-saving clubs, or placed them in "Australian" locations such as the outback or on the sporting field.

The research indicates a widely shared understanding of what it is to be Australian, which is grounded in everyday life: in real people, real places and real community groups, as well as being reflected in popular culture. Such research bears out Howard's claim that custom and long usage are the cradle of national culture. Shared cultural symbols provide people with a common vocabulary for talking about "Australian" issues and for framing the terms of debate on national issues. Talking outside this shared framework risks marginalisation, not necessarily because people will disagree with you, but rather because you simply won't be understood, or even listened to. The researchers noted in particular how rarely overt political values were mentioned in discussion. Freedom and democracy, even human rights, were there, but they were outweighed by references to mateship, owning a house, sport, having a go and other aspects of social life in Australia.

These Australians were interested in and cared deeply about Australia. John Howard knows this, and so as prime minister he talks to them about Australia in the language they share. Like them he has national heroes and is interested in national stories. He loves sport and he sees himself as embodying some of the virtues of the national character type. When he described himself to Liz Jackson as "an average Australian bloke", he listed some of his personal qualities to justify it. He was, he said, direct, unpretentious, pretty dogged and had the capacity to laugh at himself. The historian John Hirst has argued that Australian democracy is first and foremost a democracy of manners, and that Australian egalitarianism is more concerned with how people treat each other face to face, without deference or condescension, than with social structure or income equality. Being direct and unpretentious are its hallmarks.

Howard's command of the often banal idiom of everyday Australian life has been one of his greatest political assets. Because it is the language he speaks naturally, it never fails him. Even his critics had to admit he rose to the occasion in his speech at the memorial service for the Australians killed in Bali. And it gives him a flexible language of social inclusion to talk across many of the different groups and experiences that make up contemporary Australia. For a city-based politician, this language is particularly useful for talking to people who live outside the metropolitan centres in country Australia and in regional towns. It addresses aspects of Australian experience which blur class differences. And its emphasis on friendliness and hard work appeals readily to new immigrant groups.

New societies like Australia, with continuing immigration programs, need flexible national stories, ways of bringing people into the community of the nation, of reassuring newcomers that they belong and calming the anxieties of those already here about cultural and social differences. Labor accomplished this with its policy of multiculturalism, which stressed the rights of immigrant groups to maintain their cultural distinctiveness and pointed to the benefits Australia had gained from its greatly increased diversity. In the beginning, Howard rejected multiculturalism, refusing for the first few years of his prime ministership even to utter the word. For him it was Labor's word, and he associated it with a denigration of the mainstream. As he told Gerard Henderson in 1989:

> The objection I have to multiculturalism is that multiculturalism is in effect saying that it is impossible to have an Australian ethos, that it is impossible to have a common Australian culture. So we have to pretend that we are a federation of cultures and that we've got a bit from every part of the world.

Howard's preferred strategy was rather to open out the Australian ethos for others to share. Some of the quotes given above, in which Howard defines Australia's virtues, are from speeches to ethnic community organisations. The implication is that the people to whom he is speaking also share these virtues. Like Menzies' Forgotten People, though, they bear these virtues as individuals and as family members, not because they belong to a particular ethnic group. By 2003, secure and confident in his control of the centre, and with less need to distinguish himself from Labor, Howard was comfortable with "multiculturalism" and even wrote the foreword to the government's policy document *Multicultural Australia: United in Diversity*, which was, he said, "a renewed statement of our multicultural policy".

Like many Australians, particularly men, Howard identifies deeply with Australia's military past and present. As prime minister he visited the European battlefields of the two world wars where his father and grandfather fought, and he has helped to turn Anzac Day into our de facto national day. He has also, as historian Mark McKenna pointed out, associated the office of prime minister more closely with the military than any incumbent since Billy Hughes: "Wherever there is a cup of tea to be had with the military, John Howard is there." The Governor-General's role as the symbolic commander-in-chief of the armed forces has been all but usurped as the Prime Minister farewells and welcomes home the troops. McKenna counts more than thirty separate occasions between Australia's commitment to lead the United Nations InterFET Force in East Timor in 1999 and the end of 2003 when Howard mingled publicly and officiated ceremonially with the armed forces.

McKenna is writing in the wake of the Iraq war, when Howard committed Australia to the coalition of the willing despite a strong popular anti-war sentiment. Once in the war, Howard called on Australians, despite their different views of its rights and wrongs, to support the men and women of the Australian armed services. He called, that is, on feelings of national belonging to make continuing dissent seem mean-minded and marginal. McKenna says, "When John Howard cries country, invoking patriotism, he disguises political division and obscures one crucial distinction: my country is not my government." But it never has been. Of course Howard is using nationalism for political ends; what needs to be understood is why he has been able to do so with such success.

In a new country like Australia, nationalism has been particularly important for binding people together. Migrants uproot themselves from their old associations, their communal loyalties, their local and regional identities. Some of their cultural and religious institutions may be reproduced in the new land, but these are weak in comparison with the originals, and their grip over individuals loosens by the second generation. Howard's nationalism is a new-world nationalism in which, as I argued earlier, secondary associations and loyalties are conceived of as barriers to individual freedom. The nation is the only collectivity that can legitimately claim a non-negotiable loyalty.

Benedict Anderson has famously described nations as imagined communities, imagined as both inherently limited and as sovereign. Nations may have flexible boundaries, but they have boundaries nevertheless. They are particular communities, not potentially universal ones like those envisioned by some of the world's great religions. Nations can create experiences of community and commonality which people value greatly. Nations can also be used to exclude others. They can help people make sense of who they are and build reciprocal bonds between strangers – fellow citizens who will never know each other. In the twentieth century, nationalism has underpinned the redistribution of resources – effected through the welfare state – for more years than it has blown the bugles of war. The terrible carnage and appalling cruelties of last century's wars haunt political thinking about nationalism, but we need also to remember that nationalism contributed to some of that century's modest achievements.

Many intellectuals are suspicious of nationalism. They know its power to harden boundaries between people and to make them hate and kill each other. But are nations necessarily pathological? Is any appeal to a national "us" a sort of warm-up for an attack on a non-national "them", a dog-whistle letting people know they really can hate the other? I know many of Howard's critics think so, and this has in my view shaped much of the Left's commentary on his prime ministership. It is also the basic reason for its ineffectiveness, because it has made it impossible to devise successful oppositional strategies.

Because whenever he has evoked a national "us" he has been accused of really demonising a non-national "them", Howard's critics have been unable to develop any effective or plausible counter-strategies for talking to their fellow Australians. If you regard any talk of "us" as illegitimate, it is not clear to me whom you are going to talk to. Nations are not simply formed and defined by their opposition to or difference from some Other; they are also formed and defined by shared experiences and collective memories. They have centres as well as borders. As I have been arguing, Howard speaks persuasively from that centre. One does not counter him by arguing that the centre is empty, or does not exist, and that he is really only ever policing the borders. One stands in the centre with him and argues about its meanings and its responsibilities, and tells different stories to one's fellow Australians about their past and present and the bonds they share.

But nations do also have borders, and Howard has used a hard, exclusive nationalism of insiders and outsiders as well as the inclusive nationalist address to his fellow Australians which I have been describing so far. The story I have told till now is a story about Howard turning the tables on Labor to reclaim the Liberals' capacity to speak to and on behalf of the nation. But Howard was using this language of national unity for a particular aggressive purpose: to defeat Labor for the prize of government.

In my view the primal opposition which structures Howard's thinking is not Australian and un-Australian, but Liberal and Labor. It is this opposition that fuels his aggression, feeds his self-righteousness and moral indignation, and gives him the sharpness of focus to seize on the opportunities which fate presents and exploit them so ruthlessly for political advantage. Something similar was true of Keating. Both are Sydney boys, in politics from their youth. Politics channelled their adolescent energy and aggression, and they shaped their adult identities around the party polarisations, learning to become successful political warriors. Keating, though, was neither as opportunistic nor as ruthless. While aggression energised him, it could also recede and leave him with a feeling of futility, as if the prize were not worth the fight.

For Howard, if something is championed by Labor, then this is sufficient reason to oppose it, no matter what the merits of the case. To give just one obvious example, what more is needed to explain his sudden abandonment of the Liberal Party's commitment to states' rights than that all states and territories currently have Labor governments? And if people are critical of him, then he treats them as in the Labor camp, whether they are or not, and however different their views are from Labor's. Like Margaret Thatcher, there are only two possible political positions: with us or against us. From this perspective, if you are against us, you are clearly giving comfort to the enemy and so are as good as one of them. Howard's world is not dull grey at all, or even beige, as some commentators have suggested, but a vivid black and white, with enemies and supporters, bad and good, wrong and right, all lined up neatly on the two sides of the party divide. Critics putting arguments and reasoned differences are treated as opponents and shoved into the Labor camp. There is no room here for hearing a range of points of view, grappling with complexity, acknowledging uncomfortable facts. Rational nuanced debate about complex and difficult matters of public policy becomes well-nigh impossible.

Howard accused Keating and Labor of making it impossible for certain views to get a hearing, but he has done the very same thing, though to different views, and different people. There has always been an ambiguity in the Liberal Party's claim to be the party best able to represent the interests of Australia as a whole. Does the party govern on behalf of the interests and welfare of all; or in response to the views and values of the mainstream? Is it guided by considerations of the national interest or by majority opinion? The answer is that it is and can be both, and the slippage between them has always allowed Liberal leaders a certain room for political manoeuvre. Sometimes they have maintained a patrician distance, arguing that good government in the national interest requires them to take unpopular decisions; sometimes they have stayed close to commonsense public opinion.

The oppositions between national and sectional interests and between majority and minority opinions have the same formal structure of opposing part and whole, but the contents have very different political implications. One connects with the Liberal Party's patrician traditions of the responsibilities of good government, the other with democratic populism and its powerful new tools of opinion polls and focus groups to take regular soundings of the public's views, and talkback radio to broadcast them. On economic policy the Howard governments cannot be accused of populism. They have pursued unpopular taxation reform and remain committed to the privatisation of Telstra despite the opinion polls. They have listened to economic experts and drawn on academic knowledge.

In social and cultural policy and more recently in foreign policy, however, it is a different story.

Since Howard became prime minister in 1996 he has played fast and loose with the difference between the national interest and majority opinion, and with the parallel difference between sectional self-interest and minority views. What Howard has done, time and again, is to represent the opinions of people he does not agree with as the self-interested views of a section and then dismiss them as of no account. These are the elites to whom he so often refers and who he believes hold him in disdain. But if we re-describe the elites as informed public opinion we start to see what is happening, and why so many people feel alarmed, enraged even, by Howard's imperviousness to views which differ from his on the best way of advancing Australia's national interest. Those who voice informed opinions which disagree with Howard's position have been marginalised and then dismissed. Or they have been accused of attacking the mainstream, of being far more hostile and aggressive than they are, as in the for-us-or-against-us images of the culture wars.

## Howard the Fighter

Above all else, Howard is a fighter, who has spent his life fighting the chief enemy of the Liberal Party, the Labor Party. And, as the election campaigns of 1998 and 2001 show, he fights hardest when his back is to the wall. Howard is interested in war not just because he sees it as the most profound expression of our national unity and character, but also because it suits the structure of his personality and his own image of himself as a fighter. "I am the bloke", he told David Marr, "who ultimately wins the battle, and in political terms that is Churchill." He knows of course that winning an election is not the same as winning a war; yet the metaphor is telling.

In 1998 he used his championing of an unpopular tax to pull off an unlikely victory, using the GST as a vehicle to display his tough, honest and uncompromising leadership qualities. Although Labor won the national two-party preferred vote, it lost too many marginal seats, and Howard's strategy was vindicated.

In the first part of 2001, with an election due at the end of the year, Labor under Kim Beazley appeared to be cruising to victory on the backlash against the GST. It was keeping a low profile, believing that the election would be a re-run of 1996, to be lost by the government rather than won by the opposition. But in August the simmering issue of asylum seekers arriving by boat on the north coast of Australia became a national, and briefly international, crisis. The government refused landing permission to the Norwegian cargo vessel *Tampa*, which had rescued asylum seekers heading for Australia from an overloaded Indonesian fishing boat, instructing it to return them to Indonesia. The ship's captain eventually disobeyed, sailing into Australian waters where the asylum seekers were transferred from the *Tampa* to an Australian naval vessel, and then taken to hastily arranged detention centres on Nauru and Papua New Guinea — the Pacific Solution. It was policy-making on the run, in an atmosphere of fear and moral panic, with the government determined not to back down at any cost, no matter what conventions were broken or lives damaged.

Then, on September 11, the twin towers were destroyed and the war on terror unleashed. Security fears swept domestic concerns aside. Irritation with the GST seemed a minor thing in comparison with the horror of what had happened in New York, and what it revealed about the enemies of the West. A world suddenly turned black and white suits a black and white leader. His conflictual world-view seems confirmed by reality, and he offers the decisiveness the crisis seems to call for. The unfortunate asylum seekers whose boats attempted to reach Australia in the last months of 2001 sailed straight into this black and white world and became a means for Howard to continue to display his strength as the nation's leader. From champion of the nation's centre he became the defender of its borders. "We decide who comes here and the circumstances in which they come," he told the Liberal Party's campaign launch.

This assertion of national sovereignty became a key slogan in Liberal advertising material, with which it was virtually impossible for Labor to disagree.

The now notorious "children overboard" affair also occurred in this campaign. An inaccurate story about desperate asylum seekers throwing their children into the water was allowed to run, even after many people involved knew it was wrong, and without, it seems, the Prime Minister ever being told enough to incriminate him in a plan to deceive the Australian people during an election campaign. The Prime Minster said no country would want people like that, who would throw their children in the water. Subsequent enquiries raised troubling questions about the operation of the conventions meant to ensure government accountability. Many people knew the story was wrong, but no one took responsibility for ensuring that the public knew, and no one has subsequently taken responsibility for the fact that the public was not told. The incident was probably not especially significant in determining the election outcome. What it shows, though, is the ruthlessness with which Howard fights, and the focused opportunism with which he will attempt to turn whatever fate throws him to his advantage, without much concern for the long-term cost.

In this too Howard is drawing on his party's traditions, on the Liberals' capacity to fight more ruthlessly than Labor and get away with it. They seem more easily able to convince themselves of their own righteousness and of the need to do whatever it takes to keep Labor out of office, bending if not breaking the rules if it serves this ultimate purpose. The use of communism against Labor in the Cold War, forcing a constitutional crisis in 1975, ducking and weaving round the truth in the "children overboard" affair, all show this pattern to a critical eye.

Howard was born in 1939 and came to political consciousness during the battles of the Cold War when the Liberals and Menzies used communism to attack Labor's legitimacy. Labor had members on the left of the party who sympathised with Marxism's critique of capitalism, but the party eschewed revolutionary methods and was generally moderate and reformist. Nevertheless, it was divided over how to respond both to the Communist Party and to more radical ideas. Menzies' introduction of the Communist Party Dissolution Bill and the subsequent referendum exacerbated tensions in the party and the union movement, and reinforced in the minds of the electorate the association between the Labor Party and extremism. Rattling the communist can was a standard accompaniment of Liberal Party campaigning until the early 1970s, although Menzies, like Howard with "children overboard", tended to keep his distance from the really nasty stuff.

Then there was 1975 when the Liberals used the Senate to deny supply to a government with control of the lower house, breaching every convention of the Westminster system of responsible parliamentary government which the Liberals had always championed, and precipitating a constitutional crisis that destroyed the government and in the short term seriously compromised the office of the Governor-General. All this was justified in the eyes of Malcolm Fraser by the manifold faults of the Whitlam government. To this day he is publicly unrepentant about his actions: people have forgotten, he says, just how bad the Whitlam government was. Maybe, but was it so bad that it gave the Liberals the right to threaten the integrity of our parliamentary institutions? In the eyes of Fraser and his fellow Liberals it did, and we see here the way the Liberal Party can still draw upon doubts about Labor's legitimacy in order to justify a political ruthlessness which, were Labor to exhibit it, would have them screaming about power-hungry wreckers of the constitution. Labor as the newcomer has been more respectful of tradition, more careful to play by the rules than the Liberals.

Harry Evans, the distinguished Clerk of the Senate, argues that in their relationship with the parliament the Howard governments have shown little regard for the Liberal Party's tradition as an upholder of the constitution against radical change, and a defender of the checks and balances against uncontrolled executive power. The 2003 proposals for changes to the conditions governing joint sittings would have seen a massive shift in power from the parliament to the executive and been a drastic reshaping of the balance of power as it currently exists. The scheme got little support and was dropped, and as the government now has a majority in the Senate, it is unlikely to be revived. It shows, however, that the drive for power in the Howard government is stronger than the Liberal Party's traditional suspicion of the concentration of such power. I am not quite sure how to interpret this. Is it simply the long-recognised effect of holding power for so long that you start to believe in your entitlement to it? Or is it a consequence of the Liberal Party becoming an agent of radical reform, like parties of the Left once were, and so becoming, like them, hostile to constitutional constraint? There is much to be said for the latter interpretation, but I keep remembering the ruthlessness of the Liberals in the last months of 1975, their utter conviction of their own righteousness when confronting Labor, and much about Howard's appetite for power doesn't seem so new.

When the Liberals won government, Howard turned on policies, interests and groups marked as Labor's during Keating's period as prime minister: the various clamouring minorities, institutions like the ABC seen to harbour Labor sympathisers, a foreign policy too focused on Asia, the word "multiculturalism", and so on. The first casualty was Australia's indigenous people. I have already discussed the intractability of the problems posed by some indigenous political claims for the Liberal social and political imagination, but to my mind this is not enough to explain the vehemence with which indigenous people and institutions were attacked by the first Howard government. One of the new government's first acts on coming to power was to appoint a special auditor to examine organisations funded by ATSIC, and in its first budget ATSIC's funding was cut. Having got close to Labor in the heady days after the High Court's *Mabo* judgment in 1992, the indigenous leaders were regarded by the new government as in Labor's camp and so treated almost as if they were an enemy to be punished.

Howard's first term was dominated by issues not of his choosing. In particular the indigenous issues of *Wik* and the stolen generations, and the question of the republic, were hangovers from the Keating era. Howard had to develop responses, and he did so in ways which maximised the difference between his position and that of the previous government. On the republic he simply opposed it. On indigenous issues he portrayed Labor's policy as concerned mainly with symbolic gestures in contrast to his own practical approach. And he participated in the simplification of a complex historical debate about settler–indigenous history into the two opposing camps of the History Wars.

Since 1996 indigenous issues have moved from the centre of national politics to the margins. No longer critical to debates about the nation's history and its understanding of itself, they have become again an intractable problem of a small minority living on the margins of the mainstream. Indigenous leaders have retreated. Meanwhile little headway has been made on "practical" reconciliation, as indigenous Australians' life expectancy continues to lag decades behind settler Australians. But Howard's rhetoric has become less strident, his position more conciliatory. Addressing the national reconciliation planning workshop in May this year, he was at pains to lay out areas of agreement. And indigenous leaders have become more co-operative. After all, while Howard remains in office, they don't really have a choice. But they have lost power and status and now find themselves positioned more as supplicants than as partners in dialogue.

As his governments have been returned repeatedly to office, and Labor's way of defining issues has faded from public memory, Howard has gradually worked his way back to more moderate positions. Mary Kalantzis has traced this movement in relation to immigration, multiculturalism and relations with Asia. Despite the tough rhetoric of border control, immigration levels have risen substantially in recent years, with high levels of non-European migrants, and the refugee intake has remained steady. Howard has reverted to using the term "multiculturalism" and praising Australia's diversity. And in his nine years as prime minister he has made more visits to Asian countries than Hawke and Keating made between them in their thirteen. In 2004 he said it was time for a "rebalancing" back to the region. But his initial hostile polarisations have left legacies of mistrust that constrain future possibilities This is particularly the case in foreign policy where, unlike in indigenous policy, the Australian government holds very few cards. There is also the legacy of the injury inflicted on asylum seekers held for years in mandatory detention.

Successful electoral politics, I have been arguing, requires mastery of the rhetorics of both unity and division. A party leader has to make a plausible claim to represent the people as a whole while at the same time attacking the other side as fiercely as he can. In Australia, the two main parties have rhetorical repertoires for both of these tasks which are the product of their political history and have been internalised by their political activists. Howard has drawn on his party's political traditions, both in positioning himself at the centre of the nation, and in the ruthlessness with which he has played the politics of division. Today this is called wedge politics, and often presented as if it is new. But what was the DLP if not a block thrown off by a wedge driven into the heart of the Labor Party? Dancing between the rhetorics of unity and division, Howard has driven his opponents to frustrated fury. How has he got away with it? Why can't people see the contradictions and the dissemblings? Why hasn't he been held to account for his broken promises, or the way he has played upon baseless fears?

In the last section I will address these questions. I will take a long historical view of the nature of Liberal and Labor electoral support; and I will present portraits of four people who vote Liberal, playing some of the themes of this essay across their ideas and feelings about Australian politics today.

In origin the Liberals are a party of government, formed from the governing classes to fight for government in the parliament. They put into parliament men with the education, experience and connections to govern the country. Such men understand parliament, understand how to manage state finances, and have among their number men worldly and cultivated enough to represent Australia abroad with credit. The Liberals' message to the electorate is: "You can leave it to us, your government is in safe hands." Of course, since World War II the Liberals' near monopoly on men of education and manners has been broken. Gough Whitlam, a Sydney barrister and son of a senior public servant, could have been a distinguished Liberal. Instead he joined Labor during World War II as the party of reform. And the post-war expansion of secondary education brought many well-educated sons and daughters of the working class into the Labor Party. Today, there is little difference in the educational qualifications of either party's parliamentary representatives: both are composed almost entirely of the university-educated. Yet Labor has remained the party of reform, the party most likely to stir things up when its representatives get their hands on the levers of government. When, like now, Labor has no clear reform agenda, there seems little point in its existence.

After Fraser defeated Whitlam at the 1975 election, he promised to get politics off the front page. The message was that with the experienced parties of government back in power, politics would calm down, there would be no more ministerial scandals, and the economy would return to normal. Of course it didn't, and couldn't. The conditions that had sustained the long boom in the Western economies were over. Nonetheless life as usual was what was promised. Howard's claim that he would make Australians comfortable and relaxed again was a familiar one for a Liberal leader following a reforming Labor government.

## The Changing Electorate

The Liberal Party has always had to work harder for its votes than Labor. Labor in its early days displayed all the characteristics of a social movement. It was committed to fundamental social change; it called on people to identify themselves and their political interests in new ways; it unleashed a huge amount of reforming social energy and activity. The Liberals could see this, and they were frustrated by their inability to tap into a similar strength of political commitment. Whenever Labor seemed to gain the upper hand, Liberals bemoaned the weakness of their support. In 1929, when the Nationalists were defeated, *The Woman*, the monthly magazine of the Australian Women's National League, editorialised:

> We see the Labor party machine ruthlessly but efficiently crushing factions and oppositions and we lament the inadequacy of our own machinery ... Effective machinery is only the outward and visible sign of the spirit that gives it birth ... Have we no clarion call? Are there no inspiring principles that would give us that exuberant vitality that ensures ultimate victory?

For a brief moment between 1946 and 1949, Liberals spoke confidently of "the Liberal movement", but its energy soon dissipated in the paranoia of the Cold War, and in 1957 Harold Holt voiced the now-familiar lament: "We have never experienced the fervour and unquestioning loyalty which Labour [sic] could confidently expect for so many of its better years from a great mass of people." But in 1957 the Liberals had Menzies, and with such a leader the absence of fervour was not an electoral problem.

In 1967 Don Aitkin commenced a survey of Australians' party identification. The first national study using the new mass survey techniques and computers to analyse the results, it provides a benchmark against which to measure subsequent changes in party identification. In 1967 Aitkin found that 37 per cent of people who thought of themselves as Labor supporters described their support as "very strong" compared with only

27 per cent for the Liberals. Since then the number of loyal supporters has declined for both parties. In 1996 only 19 per cent of the identifiers of both parties described their support as very strong. The key point here is that Labor's decline was off a much higher base, and so it now had to work harder for its primary vote than in the late 1960s.

This is linked to another change in the electorate since the 1960s. Along with the decline in loyal supporters, the electorate is now generally better informed about politics and more interested. Aitkin found increased interest in politics between his first survey in the late 1960s and his second in the 1970s. Those reporting that they now took an active interest in politics had increased from 27 per cent to 43 per cent, and the numbers of the apathetic were down from 35 per cent to 20 per cent. Aitkin put this down to two things: the politicisation of women, resulting both from their increasing levels of education and the new feminist agenda, and the harder economic times. The first survey was conducted in the Indian summer of the long boom, when unemployment seemed a thing of the past and families could still be raised on one male wage. By 1979 the boom was over, though the implications of this for the economy as a whole, and for individual Australians, were only just starting to sink in. People were more aware of politics, but also more pessimistic and cynical.

As political interest has increased, strong partisanship has declined. Again this has had bigger implications for Labor than for the Liberals. In 1967 Liberal identifiers were likely to be more interested in politics than Labor identifiers: one Labor identifier in seven was both strongly committed to Labor and had little interest in day-to-day politics; the Liberal equivalent was one in thirteen. As Aitkin said, these findings were of great moment. A person with strong ties to a party but with little interest in politics is unreachable, and in the 1960s Labor had two and a half times more of these supporters than did the Liberals. For those loyal Labor supporters who knew almost nothing about politics, party loyalty was a consequence of their position in the social structure: these were blue-collar manual workers and their wives, trade union members, who lived in working-class suburbs and regional mining towns. Voting Labor was an aspect of their identity, and no more open to change than was their religion or their football team.

Although the Liberals had a core support base in the white-collar middle class, they always rejected the idea that this support was based on economic self-interest. They believed that voters had to be won, persuaded to vote Liberal through appeal to reason and principle, or, if this failed, to fear. As Aitkin's evidence indicates, they were right to believe this. As a consequence they had to become more skilled at electoral politics. And they still are. They are thus better positioned than Labor to win elections in a fundamentally changed electorate where the core support for both parties is down, and general interest in politics is up.

Aitkin found softening party identification in the late 1970s, but the sharp slump seems to have occurred during the 1980s. As both Liberal and Labor signed up to economic rationalism, confidence in the parties and in political institutions more generally was badly dented. Until 1987 the combined primary vote for the major parties (including the Nationals) was above 90 per cent; in 1993 it was below 80 per cent.

The policies and behaviour of the parties during the 1980s were important in this, but so too were other factors. Australia's social structure was changing. The solid rock of occupational identity on which the party system was founded was being eroded: people changed jobs across a lifetime and there was more casual employment. Such processes have continued to gather momentum. Income no longer follows education as closely as it once did, with some blue-collar tradesmen earning more than tertiary-educated professionals. The social movement issues of gender, race and ethnicity have politicised other aspects of people's social identity. And continuing migration brings in new cohorts of adult voters each year whose allegiance must be courted. Australian society is thus infinitely more complex than it was in the first decades of the twentieth century when the party system was formed. Social structure doesn't deliver solid blocks of electoral support in the way it once did, and the Liberals, who never relied on social structure to the same degree as Labor have been quicker to adapt.

As well, the Liberals' language of individualism connects with changes in the way people now experience their lives. More and more, people perceive their lives as individual projects rather than lived-out fates. Consumerism, the culture of authenticity and self-expression, changing family structures, a greater emphasis on individual rights and a recognition of cultural diversity – all these tendencies reconstruct society as the amalgam of freely choosing individuals championed by the Liberal Party.

New parties have also played a part. Minor parties – the Greens, Democrats, Family First and One Nation – have arisen to give the people loosened from the major parties somewhere else to go. Even though many of these voters are forced back to the major parties when a minor party collapses, as has happened with One Nation and the Democrats, party allegiances have been weakened. The electorate now contains many voters who could be described as "softly committed": those who split their vote between the House of Representatives and the Senate; who vote differently in state and federal elections; who give their first preferences to minor parties; who decide during the election campaign mainly on the basis of leadership; who do support one of the majors, but change their vote on occasion, perhaps over an issue, or a candidate. And then there are the alienated who use their vote to punish the party that annoys them most rather than to express a clear preference. And last are the airheads and drongos who know nothing and care less. All except the lattter are voters to be wooed and won by the party with the superior political skills. Leadership, the campaign, particular issues both local and national, and the quality of candidates have all become more significant in determining the outcome of an election than they once were. John Howard's message to his party during each election campaign, that voters can't be taken for granted and that the election has to be won, shows an astute understanding of the nature of the less partisan, better informed, increasingly disaggregated contemporary electorate.

## Ordinary People Who Vote Liberal

As Howard has won election after election, there has been a great deal of speculation about what his victory shows about the Australian people, their grievances, their xenophobia, their racism even, their self-centred materialism. Most of this speculation has come from left commentators such as Philip Adams, and from Labor supporters more generally, looking for explanations in the nature of the people for Labor's electoral failures, rather than to Labor's own manifest political problems. Such talk always ignores the large numbers of people who do not vote for the Coalition — almost 50 per cent of the country, after all. It also massively oversimplifies the nature of Liberal support, and all the contradictory views and impulses that are resolved in each person's decision about how to vote. Some people have undoubtedly changed their vote because of fear, some because of the government's policy on asylum seekers, but many people have kept on voting Liberal for the sorts of reasons they have always voted Liberal.

This last part of the essay is my attempt to defend the Australian people against some of the accusations that have been levelled against them because Howard has kept winning elections. I look at four people who have mostly voted Liberal. The first two, a self-employed tradesman and a tradesman's wife, are prosperous small-business people from the Liberal heartland. The third is a low-level public sector clerk who has not found life so easy and has little time for politicians. The fourth is a young casual worker whose life revolves around an inner-city nightclub and who has been attracted to Howard's tough stance on border control. These people were interviewed for a research project on the politics of ordinary Australians, and their attitude to the parties was only a small part of what was discussed. But the interviews give an insight into some of the reasons people vote Liberal, and also into the way in which Howard has connected with these reasons.

The interviews were long, repeated and open-ended, each person being interviewed for somewhere between six and ten hours. Talking with people for such a long time gives a larger picture of how important politics is for them. The interviews aimed not just to get at the faces behind the views, but to reveal aspects of people's political outlook that are barely visible in quantitative measures like opinion polls.

### i. *Wayne Doherty*

Wayne Doherty and Caroline Walker (our second interviewee) are both hard-working, successful small-business people. Wayne is a motor mechanic, and Caroline runs the office for her husband's business in the building trade. They live full, busy lives in known, densely networked worlds of work, family and friends, and they spend very little time thinking about politics. They live what we might describe as embedded lives, in which politics is almost an afterthought in a society and economy that, as far as they are concerned, is working well and throws up few challenges to their established ideas about life or Australia.

Wayne is a master tradesman in his late thirties. When he was first interviewed in 1988, he was twenty-four and already running his own business – a small specialised business in the car industry. Fifteen years later the business "is rolling along nicely" and he employs two apprentices, which gives him a little more time to indulge his passion for motor sport. He has moved out of the family home, and is married with three children. His wife works, they are paying off the house, and they live in a suburb not far from where he grew up.

Wayne loves his work. He is skilled with his hands and enjoys practising his trade and teaching it to others. For him work is what being an adult is all about and he cannot imagine life without it – sitting at home all day. Two mates of his without work found themselves in "nervous breakdown–type situations". Unsurprisingly, Wayne has no sympathy for young people who take the dole, though he says it's a different story for the people over fifty who've already had to work. As far as he's concerned, the work is there – it's just a matter of "how you motivate yourself". He thinks the problem of unemployment could be simply solved by removing the dole. He divides the world into the active and the lazy, and sees removing the props as the only way to solve the problem of laziness. He does voice some of the conventional complaints about his money being used to support people who don't work, but this is not the heart of his objection. It is rather that he cannot imagine why anyone would not want to work, or how a meaningful life could be lived without it.

Wayne's belief that work is the key to life is based on his own experience. He has always worked hard, as did his parents before him. "Dole was a dirty word in our house." His parents taught him the value of hard work – by making him work for his first car, for example, rather than giving it to him. But they always backed him too, as when his father let him set up his first workshop in his car yard, organised an apprenticeship for him through a business contact, and gave him much practical advice in the first years of his business – from how to psyche out prospective employees to how to organise the job sheets and the books. "Getting on is 50 per cent who you know," says Wayne.

To Wayne his life is self-evidently the result of his own and his family's efforts; the policy settings and social and economic structures that sustain it are largely invisible. He has not had to look to the government for help himself, and he cannot imagine circumstances in which he might have to rely on the government in the future. In 1988 he was asked about the possible impact of a change of federal government. He thought a Liberal government might cut down the paperwork for small business a bit, and might improve the way the Apprenticeship Board was run, "but that's about it really." And fifteen years later that was about it. He was pleased with the GST, which had reduced the paperwork for a business like his, but otherwise he couldn't nominate any issues from the intervening years that he'd taken much notice of.

> I'm not really into that sort of stuff. Politics is only a conversation piece really. They can bring something up, talk about it, pass a bill. They can do what they like But nothing ever really changes that

much. I don't think they've ever done anything massive other than send people to war.

Wayne votes Liberal. As Graeme Davison has argued in *Car Wars*, the Liberal Party has always been the party of the motor trade, supporting the freedom, choice and individuality of private transport against the bureaucratic regulation and mass delivery of the public system. As a third-generation member of that trade, Wayne supports the Liberal Party as the party of small business, though not with a great deal of enthusiasm. It is a traditional, family-based association of the sort that political sociologists once saw as the foundation of Australia's stable party system, when family and socio-economic location bequeathed life-long party affiliations.

### ii. *Caroline Walker*

Our tradesman's wife, Caroline Walker, professes even less interest in politics than Wayne. In 1988 she was combining the roles of housewife and mother with doing the books for her husband. Fifteen years later the children were grown up and she was running the office in her husband's much-expanded business. She was sixty and planning to retire in three years' time. When asked in 2003 if there were any issues in federal or state politics that concerned her, she replied:

> Not me, because I tend to go along with whatever the decision is that's made. It's a bit beyond me. I'm only a little homebody. I'm happy to do what I do, administering the office. If it's finances I'm happy to delve into it. Oh I read about it and I change my mind from election to election when I'm voting because I tend to look at the leader. I always think the leader of the ship makes a big difference. Who did I vote for last time? Probably little Johnny Howard, the Liberals, which I've probably done mostly.

Notice here how Caroline expresses her decision to vote for the Liberals. She doesn't say "I'm a Liberal" as if it were a fixed aspect of her social identity, but presents it as a conscious choice in which at each election she considers the matter, and mostly comes to the same conclusion.

Caroline left school after Form Three to train as a bookkeeper, and was conscious of her lack of formal education. Like most people, she avoided situations which made her feel inadequate, either intellectually or emotionally. Politics raised questions about things beyond her known world, and out of reach of any effective action by her. So she chose a leader and left him to it. For Caroline politics is not even a conversation piece, and several times she complained about people who want to talk about politics at social occasions: "I like pleasant nice chatter. They get into too many fights and get a bit hypo with their points of view." Caroline sees politics as unruly, "full of fighting and squabbling and telling fibs", but apart from a few local issues she displays no sense that it impinges on her day-to-day life.

The only political issues that grabbed her attention were local ones – a proposal to build a new supermarket, some old trees that had been chopped down to widen a road. She was very difficult to draw on the standard range of issues that respondents were asked about. As she says, "I don't have strong views on things unless I know first-hand." Whenever she did offer an opinion, it was always backed up by reference to something that had happened to her. She did not trust second-hand reports, and she certainly did not trust the media. She gave examples of the way the local paper had misreported the words of her husband. Caroline is someone who values competence, and part of her reluctance to offer opinions may have been a caution about appearing ill-informed to the person from the university who was interviewing her. But there was something more. Her lack of political engagement seemed to be part of a broader lack of curiosity about how other people live. Asked in 2003 whether Australia had become more or less fair since she was last interviewed in 1988, she replied:

> Well, I think there's still opportunity for people. I believe everything is hard work and people are wanting to do less and less for

more money. And I think people generally are much more comfortable than they've ever been, but perhaps I'm in a different environment. I don't mix with people that are the dole people. I just don't know any. It's not that I deliberately don't but I just don't happen to know how hard it is for them. But the people around me I know are all very comfortable.

Essentially her answer is that she and the people she knows have done well. She supposes there must be people who are battling, "but you don't know what their circumstances are, why they're battling, that's what I always want to know. They're not battling for no reason. There are jobs out there." Caroline is softer than Wayne in her attitudes, more prepared to imagine that some people are doing it hard, but she has no more imagination than he does of what this might mean, nor interest in the circumstances that might have led people to their plights. That is, like Wayne, she looks at the social world through the lens of a taken-for-granted individualism based in the commonsense of her known world.

Politics has to affect her directly – to impinge on her daily life and concerns – for it to warrant any attention. "I'm very insular. I just focus on what we're doing. I probably should look outside the square, but I don't." Not looking outside the square, Caroline does not seem to have reflected much on the reasons why she and the people she knows are now so comfortable. For example, the business she administers has benefited from privatisation, winning contracts for tasks that would once have been done by government departments. Caroline is better informed about politics than she lets on, but she does not invest in it emotionally and refuses to let it upset the calm of her daily life. Her second set of interviews took place shortly after the start of the Iraq war.

> Wars horrify me. I'm too scared to even read about it, like the war in Iraq. It just saddens me that those children are being left without parents, or maimed. It chews me up. I can't watch it on television.

I hate it. That's why I don't take a lot of notice. I insulate myself against things I don't like, perhaps ... Anyway, my little bit of say wouldn't go too far.

On refugees she gave a confused and ambiguous response. She'd once read a popular novel about Afghanistan, and was horrified by the barbaric cruelty of some of the punishments and the social position of women.

I do believe we should accept them, but they've really got to come the right way. There's got to be rules and regulations, and a correct way of doing things. We'd have the country flooded with them if we don't have some sort of rules and regulations. But I do feel for them. I mean, if they're brave enough to uproot themselves from their own country like that. They're often quite well-educated people that are doing it. They must be desperate.

Here Caroline swings between compassion and the fear of loss of control, showing just how much room Howard in fact had to move in developing his political response to asylum seekers. A person like Caroline could have been moved either way, depending on how the leader played the issue.

The place where Caroline feels most herself is her lounge room, as she sits in front of a fire on a winter's afternoon looking out onto her garden. Here, she said in 1988, she felt "relaxed and comfortable", with no one to judge her or find her wanting, and nothing to disturb her tranquillity. Wayne and Caroline live at the heart of John Howard's projected Australia. Both see their lives as the result of their own efforts. They work hard and are confident and successful in their businesses, with little overt sense of grievance or resentment. Life has gone smoothly for them, and they still live close to the people and places of their childhoods. Family and friends are close to hand for help if needed. Wayne boasts that he always knows whom to ring to fix things up, and Caroline and her husband are well connected in their local community. Secure and well-resourced both financially and socially, neither feels that anything the government might do could affect much but the edges of their lives; a little bit more or less inconvenience or expense is the most they expect, and certainly all that they want.

The most they can be accused of is smugness. Neither is interested in the lives of those who demand or need more from politics. Both believe that Australia has plenty of work for those who want it, and have stories to back this up, of offering someone a job who turned it down, or of putting on new people. Living at the centre of their worlds, they look out as far as they need to but have only a patchy sense of the society and the economy as a whole. Social problems present themselves as the problems of individuals and they see the solutions to these problems as largely in these individuals' hands. They are not unduly harsh, nor quick to blame. They are not even unsympathetic, and both have helped friends in need. But they cannot conceive of themselves being in situations where they would not be able to marshal the resources they need to solve their problems — except in the area of health. And so they cannot really imagine how others can be in such situations. For both it thus boils down to the question of individual attitude. This is not a case of blaming the victim but of the inability to imagine ever being a victim. The Liberals have always appealed to people like Caroline and Wayne, offering themselves as the party best able to govern, least likely to shake things up, and making the least demand on their attention.

### iii. Lois McGuinness

Our third person, Lois, is quite different. She can imagine being a victim, and a better, fairer world where people like her would get more, but she doesn't expect that to happen so she can see little point in believing politicians who make promises. Lois was a public sector clerk in her late forties when she was interviewed in 1988. She was the eldest of a big family and had grown up in the country. Neither of her parents had taken much interest in her education, and when she wasn't married as expected by her mid-twenties she had no map of how to live. She worked in low-paid jobs which gave her little job satisfaction, travelled a lot, played sport and generally made the best of what her life offered. It is certainly not her commitment to work that leads her to prefer the Liberals to Labor. She votes the way her conservative parents did, but keeps her party preference to herself.

Although she had worked for the government for much of her life, Lois placed little faith in politics.

> The government that is in is the government that's governing. Whether you believe in it or not is really irrelevant. It is going to happen. There's no perfect government, and there's no perfect policy. If a new government gets in, it can't overnight make everything perfect. Surely the general person can see that some of the things they pledge are just not possible.

Politicians make Lois's skin crawl. She is quiet and unassuming, and the self-display of a life in public politics grates against something deep in Lois's way of being in the world.

> My worst fear for all these elections is that they all make such big idiots of themselves … I personally don't like Hawke very much. I don't trust him. There's something about his charisma that makes me sort of cringe every time I see him.
>
> And Howard just thinks he's so fantastic and so does his wife. I mean he's an embarrassment. (This comment was made in 1988.)

For Lois politics is a world of illusion and self-display, which is more likely to upset the hold she has on her happiness and peace of mind than to enhance it. Only once in more than twelve hours of interviews did Lois depart from her fatalistic resignation. Asked a general question about the fairness of the Australian political system, she complained about percentage pay rises, the way the person at the top gets more from them than does the person at the bottom, who needs the rise more.

What about me? Being pretty low down there on the scale myself, what hope have I got of ever getting ahead? These people down the bottom have got the same ambitions as the people at the top. It's just maybe they had the opportunities early in life. OK, a lot of people at the top have worked hard to get there, and a lot of people at the bottom have only themselves to blame, but not all of them have. There are a lot of people who are down there through circumstances and the government has not helped them to get out of being down there.

Here is a sense of grievance that could draw Lois towards politics, but to her it's a siren call.

I don't believe politicians. This one's saying this, this one's saying that. But I know darn well they don't have all the money to do all these things they say they do. It's just looking at ways to get votes. Not what is best for Australia. There are so many people that are vulnerable, that they'll believe them all. I mean every election's been exactly the same. I must admit I turn off. Because I don't believe any of them.

To Lois, what makes you vulnerable is not need, but rather the belief that politicians might be able to make a fundamental difference to your life situation. Instead of yielding to such beliefs, one should just get on and "make the best of things". Lois works hard to hang on to the sense that her life is OK, and if this involves damping down expectations, then so be it. It is better than finding yourself filled up with negative emotions like disappointment, anger, envy, resentment. Lois is thus unreachable by the sort of politics of hope to which Labor can appeal at its reforming best, but also by the politics of grievance to which the radical populist ends of both right and left at times appeal.

Lois does not believe in complaining, and while she is generally positive about multiculturalism, she has no time for migrants who complain about Australia.

My reaction to them is – you've come to our country, we've accepted you, change your ways, be like us. Sometimes I really feel like screaming at them and saying, "Listen, you know you're very lucky. You've come to a good life out here and it's what you make it." So they should just keep quiet and get on with living and make the most of the opportunities that this country's offered them. Because they are honoured to have been let into our country.

Keep quiet, get on with living, and make the most of the opportunities Australia offers. This is Lois's recipe for a reasonable life. It is not the expression of intolerance towards people who are different, nor is it complacency born of an easy life. Rather it is an achievement of her own. And like most people, she uses her own life and her own experiences as the yardstick by which she judges others. Nevertheless this quote tells us a great deal about how Lois views immigrants and understands multiculturalism. The pronouns she uses are "us" and "them", just as they are in her more positive comments about multiculturalism and immigration:

Well before the Europeans started coming we were very plain ordinary living people. I don't think the Europeans and the Asians have done us any harm. They haven't come out here to try to govern us, or to take our money away from us. They've come here to live and they've adjusted. They live the Australian way of life but they've brought their cultures, and we tend to have adapted to them, especially in our eating habits. I dread to think what we'd be eating now if there hadn't been any immigration. We'd be very plain, ordinary eating people.

Lois is unselfconscious in her use of "us" and "them", positioning herself as the host. The conventions of hospitality are important to her, and one of the things she praises immigrants for, along with their hard work, is their hospitality. "They welcome you into their homes, and treat you as a guest." The big sin is to complain. We have already seen how Lois rejects the resort to complaint as a way of managing the disappointments of her life. But it is also what "they" are complaining about that drives her almost to screaming point. They are complaining about Australia. Australia and having been born Australian are the great joys of Lois's life.

A sense of national pride detached from the country's political institutions has often been seen as a characteristic of Australian political culture. Whereas Lois works hard to distance the illusory promises of politics and its disturbing invitations to hope or grievance, talking about Australia is a different matter. It brings a smile to her face and is a continuing source of pride and pleasure. Where governments may let you down, Australia never does.

> We are the lucky country. We have vast open spaces and we are very warm hospitable people. We have lovely beaches, ski resorts, tourist attractions galore. Best restaurants in the world. Wineries everywhere. Top class accommodation. Good shopping. The Opera House, the Queensland beaches, Beautiful one day and perfect the next.

Lois identifies deeply with Australia. Asked in 2004 about changes since she was last interviewed, she described with pleasure improvements she has noticed in her travels round the country – development of the wharves in Echuca, beautiful landscaping projects along the Great Ocean Road, new bike and walking tracks around Melbourne, the improvements to Southbank and around Albert Park. These improvements are all ones in the general public amenity, and Lois described them with a real sense of ownership. These are places she would be proud to show to overseas visitors.

Australia is a psychological resource for Lois which buoys up her sense of good fortune and soothes the disappointing and limited aspects of her life. And she loves sport. Work had never given her much and she took a package just before she turned fifty-five. Sport is the centre of her life and she places it at the centre of the nation. Asked what brings Australia together, she didn't hesitate – "Sport."

Australians are a sporting people. We're very lucky to have the Institute of Sport up in Canberra. I don't know who thought of it, but there was a recognition of the fact that if we don't have it, our Olympians and young sporting people won't ever have the opportunity. When I saw the Olympians arrive home in Sydney and walk off that plane, the tears were just rolling down my face. There were just so many of them, loads and loads and loads of people. It was just so wonderful to think of all those people over there in Athens and what they've achieved.

One of the big regrets of Lois's life is that she discovered her talent for sport too late to become really good at it, but her strong sense of national identity enables her to take pride in the successes of these young Olympians almost as if they were her own children.

### iv. Marc Dorovic

In 2004 Marc was twenty-five and living with his mother in Keilor. The only child of Croatian immigrants who came to Australia in the mid-1970s, he was born here shortly after their arrival. Like most young immigrants, his parents had come to Australia for a better life, but things did not work out well. Their marriage foundered and his mother injured her back working as a nurse. In his late teens Marc and his mother had moved from the vibrant inner city where he grew up to the suburbs, which he regarded as unutterably boring, fine for retirement, but no place for a young man about town. Marc's mother kept some connections with the Croatian community, but this didn't interest him and he hopes one day to move back to the inner city. Well-groomed and dressed in fashionable street gear, Marc spends little time at home, preferring to walk the streets of the inner-city listening to his music, or to sit in cafes and bars. He looks like he might be a member of the progressive left caffe-latte set, but in fact he votes for John Howard.

Although Marc doesn't like Keilor, he has few options but to live with his mother. He did not do well at school, nor at a TAFE hospitality course, and since completing the latter he has had a series of casual and part-time jobs. The longest was as a telemarketer. This lasted nearly three years, but the hours were never permanent and he lost the job when the company moved interstate. Although he has at times contacted Centrelink for help in finding work, he has refused to take the dole.

> I think I would have gotten more lazy in finding a job if I had started
> getting the dole. Being a statistic, as in a person who is on the dole,
> I wouldn't have been comfortable with that.

Between jobs his mother gave him spending money, which he later paid back.

So long as he keeps living with his mother, Marc works enough to stop himself slipping into the obscurity of welfare, but apart from this, work gives him little. He has made no friends from his various jobs, and their short-term, casual nature has made it impossible for him to plan any sort of future. In contrast to many immigrants and their children, for whom hard work is the major means of orienting themselves to their new country, Marc's commitment to work is low. And it certainly does not give him an occupational identity, or a stable vantage point from which to build a political outlook.

Not that this worries Marc. He doesn't see himself as needing anything much from government. The economy is going OK and he has always been able to get a job. He has minor complaints about public transport since it's been privatised, but is not interested in reflecting on the reasons for or the more general consequences of privatisation. And on most political issues he doesn't know enough to make a judgment.

> For me to think about something like the immigration program
> would be too hard, too much to grasp. So I'll leave it in the Aust-
> ralian government's hands. That's why we vote. We've got the
> power to vote, so hopefully we can get the right people to do the
> right job.

Apart from his mother, for whom he does feel a genuine sense of responsibility, the only anchor in Marc's life is the nightclub where he has been spending his weekends for the past five years. Nightclubs, he says, have a bad reputation, but people don't really know about them. The one he goes to is "small and tight-knit, a really good place. People look after you there, you can trust them." There he meets people who seem to be doing well, "managers, responsible people with well-established lifestyles", and Marc enjoys socialising with them. He frequently describes himself as "lazy" and "a bit immature", with no clear goal in life. Compared with some of the people he sees at the nightclub, he doesn't yet have what he regards as a viable adult identity, nor much idea of how he could get one.

The nightclub is Marc's community, and he has invested a lot of time, money and emotions in it. But as a community it has its limitations. It is expensive, and he can't really afford the amount of time he spends there. Then there are the drugs, which mean that you can't always tell if friendliness is genuine or a result of substances. Marc has had his own problems with drugs, which messed with his emotions and made him depressed. But despite the drawbacks of the nightclub, Marc has no other long-lasting point of connection with a broader social world.

As he goes about his day-to-day and night-time life, Marc takes very little interest in politics. He doesn't know much about the nation's political institutions, and has no views on most issues. He gives two explanations for this. The first is that as the economy is basically OK he can forget about the government – this despite his objectively vulnerable position in the job market. The second is that he doesn't have the information, which is perhaps a way of excusing his ignorance to the interviewer. Politics does not present itself to Marc as an arena in which identifiable interests and values compete for resources and attention. More than this, he has no stable point of identification in his own life from which he could start to build a sense of politics. He does not identify with the suburbs where he lives; nor has his immigrant background or his work history given him a community of stakeholders and some shared opponents; and his main point of identification, the nightclub, is scarcely a political space.

The only political issues that sparked Marc's interest were external threats. Terrorism loomed large, and he linked it to immigration and security issues, as Howard had done in the 2001 election campaign:

> If we're going to be getting immigrants, the simple fact is that if they're terrorists and if they're not telling us about it then who's to say if we won't be the next September 11. So the main thing is we've got to start looking after ourselves.

He was asked what he thought about accusations that Howard had not told the truth about Iraq having weapons of mass destruction. The lies, he said, did not worry him, "if your heart's in the right place in wanting to deal with terrorism". And he strongly supported the American alliance, "considering the fact that they are the most powerful country in the world".

For Marc the only thing that mattered about a political leader was that they would "take care of Australia", because "you have to look after yourself." On this score Marc thought Howard was doing well. He wholeheartedly supported his tough stance on asylum seekers.

> I really think he's a good leader. He takes the hard decisions. He's not much of an attractive guy, in fact the main thing I've got against him is his looks. But people look past that and say well it doesn't matter if he's attractive, or if he's sucking up to all the big people around the world, we're still voting for him because he's a true Australian, no matter what.

Howard's skill in identifying himself with images and symbols of Australianness which connect with people's everyday life and experience has been one of the themes of this essay. But unpretentiousness and informality of manners, the nation's obsession with sport, Australia's military traditions and pioneering history – none of this had any resonance for Marc.

What it means to be Australian? I suppose people don't really think about it because it's so diverse. To me what it means to be Australian is plenty of opportunity. It means for me I can have any sort of lifestyle I choose. Lots of freedom. As long as you've got a head on your shoulders and you're not out there to hurt anyone, lots of freedom.

This is a strikingly contentless description. Australia for Marc is a space more than a place. Its people have no special characteristics, and he doesn't even mention the great outdoors. I argued earlier in this essay that to understand the way Howard has played the politics of the nation, we have to remember that nations have both centres and borders. A passionate nationalist like Lois will respond to Howard's depiction of the nation's centre as filled with easygoing sports-loving people who enjoy what this great land has to offer. But for Marc Australia is not much more than a space with a border, and politics is stripped back to its most basic function, the use of state power to maintain territorial integrity. Walking the city streets, imagining he is free, the only thing Marc can think to demand of politicians is that they protect the country's borders.

Our four voters display a continuum of support for the Liberals, and help us to think about the different layers of experience on which Howard has drawn since 1996. Marc's connection to Howard and the Liberals is the most tenuous. Were economic conditions to change and jobs become harder to find, he might well decide that the tasks of government are more than just protecting the border. With no occupational or other social identification to anchor his political choices, his vote would come up for grabs in the new fluid electorate. Lois connects with Howard's nationalism – his recognition of the deep pleasures people draw from being Australian. Her distrust of the politics of either hope or grievance will inure her to any Labor revival, but she reminds Labor that it must have a national story to tell if it is to reach across people's distrust of politics to connect with their sense of shared experiences and obligations. Wayne and Caroline are the solid core of Howard's support, the small-business heart of his Liberal Party.

Every successful political leader has a core group, a personal social heartland, whose values and experiences he or she elevates to the national stage and makes the centre of the national story. This must be done skilfully, in ways that are not too exclusive, but it remains a source of passion, a reference point which anchors the purpose and hard slog of a political life deep in the self and the formative relationships of childhood. For Howard this group is small business.

Howard is the Australian prime minister who has been closest to the values and experience of small business. His father, who ran a petrol station, worked the long, long hours characteristic of the service sector; John, his youngest son, identified deeply with small business's problems and took on small business's enemies as his own – an interfering socialist government and the trade unions. He remembers with glee the night the Liberals won the 1949 election and the family burnt the ration books.

Menzies was also the son of shopkeepers, but their vision was broader and their enemies less vivid. Local and state politics engaged much of his father's time and energies, and onto this commitment to community involvement Menzies grafted the values of the professional middle class with their belief in a liberal education and culture. Sport interested him, but it was not his only source of recreational pleasure, and he took pride in Australia's writers and artists as well as its cricketers. He supported and understood the suburban culture that prospered during his government, but it did not set the limits of his own cultural interests. Outside of his work and his family, Howard by contrast seems to have only sport. In this he is like Wayne, and many other Australian men.

In the much-written-about divide between Howard and the so-called elites, it seems to me that Howard's limited cultural interests have been a significant factor. Differences in values, particularly around issues of race, have also been important for many people, but much criticism of Howard draws on the anti-suburban discourse that took shape in the 1950s, railing against the complacent conformism attributed to those years, before the 1960s loosened conventional morality and before Whitlam gave us a national policy for the arts. Howard horrifies many of the cultural and educational elites in part because he has no interest in them and in the contribution they make to national life. And his government's cultural and higher education policies have reflected that.

Until now, Howard's political career has been marked by the political skills and quick-footedness which, I have argued, are part of the Liberals' political heritage as a successful parliamentary party. Howard has been able to turn and tack as he has reached out to blue-collar voters, farmers, first-home buyers, families with mortgages, women with young children who want to stay at home, old people whose incomes have been affected by low interest rates, and so on. Out of these groups he has put together winning coalitions. On some things he has stood firm in the face of widespread opposition: the GST, which nearly cost him the 1998 election, and the war in Iraq. He is now standing firm on another – the industrial relations legislation that aims to free small business from trade unions once and for all. It is legislation which, whatever the rhetoric of choice and flexibility, decisively tilts the balance of power to employers in a situation where it is not obvious that unions are any longer a problem for economic growth. And it creates a unified national system in defiance of the Liberal Party's commitment to federalism and states' rights. It is, though, legislation for Howard's small-business heartland, his special group, the service of which is the emotional point of his political career. Will this be the point at which his political instincts fail him?

If politics followed fictional forms, history's irony would make this legislation the bridge too far which marked Howard's loss of political judgment. It would be like Chifley's disastrous decision to nationalise the banks, which was the beginning of the end for Labor's post-war government, and which Howard's family celebrated in 1949. In his attack on the banks, Chifley was fighting the battles of the past, rooted in the experiences of the 1890s. Banking had already been brought under government regulation and his proposal for nationalisation was a radical overreaching. Similarly, today's unions are weak and have already accepted much of the workplace reform agenda. Australians do not like ideologues and extremists, though they are prepared to tolerate pain and radical reform when they can be convinced that these are unavoidable. Howard has made much of the need for balance, of finding and holding the moderate, consensual middle. Will this legislation mark his loss of political acumen as his small-business heart imagines the unions of today are the unions of the 1950s? Or will he, as he has before, bow and bend before sustained political pressure, keeping his government to the moderate middle of national experience?

# SOURCES

This essay draws on positions argued at much greater length in my two books on the history of the Liberal Party, *Robert Menzies' Forgotten People* and *Australian Liberals and the Moral Middle Class*, as well as on developments in Australian politics since the latter was finished in 2002. I hope it may lead some new readers to those books. In the final section I discuss some interviews from a research project on contemporary political outlooks, and I wish to acknowledge the contribution to this of my La Trobe University colleagues on the project, Anthony Moran, Uldis Ozolins and Guinevere Threlkeld, as well as the anonymous respondents.

1       Footage of Menzies: "The Ming Dynasty", *Hindsight*, ABC, 1990.

3       "We took the name Liberal": Robert Menzies, *Afternoon Light*, Cassell, Melbourne, 1967, p. 286.

4       "the man who says 'No'": Menzies' opening speech to the Albury conference to discuss the formation of the new party, 14 October 1944, cited in Graeme Starr, *The Liberal Party of Australia: A Documentary History*, Drummond/Heinemann, Richmond, 1980, p. 90.

5       Deakin: The Liberal Party, Leaflet, NLA MS 1924/18/51, p. 7.

5       Howard: "The Liberal Tradition: the beliefs and values which guide the federal government", 1996 Robert Menzies Lecture, in A. Gregory (ed.), *The Menzies Lectures*, Sir Robert Menzies Lecture Trust, Melbourne, 1999.

5       Kemp: *Australian*, 18 March 1992.

6       Robert Doyle quote from Kathy Evans, "Outraged of Malvern", *Sunday Age*, 30 May 2004, p. 8.

8       Development over the next decade of procedures: see Ross McMullin, *The Light on the Hill: The Australian Labor Party, 1891–1991*, Oxford University Press, Melbourne, 1991, Chapters 1–3.

8       Deakin: *Age*, 2 February 1904.

10      Lyons' resignation speech: Commonwealth Parliamentary Debates, vol. 128, 13 March 1931, pp. 229–38.

11      Menzies' "Forgotten People" speech was first published in a pamphlet by Robertson and Mullins of Melbourne shortly after it was delivered. It was then published as the title essay in a collection of Menzies' speeches published by Angus & Robertson, Sydney in 1943. I reproduced the speech in my *Robert Menzies' Forgotten People*, Macmillan, Sydney, 1992, pp. 3–14.

12      Menzies on his own class origins: interview with Ken Taylor recorded for the ABC, 25 February 1965, copy in oral history collection, NLA, TRC 1169/294–4.

13     John Stuart Mill, "On Representative Government", *Collected Works of John Stuart Mill*, vol. 19, edited by J.M. Robson, University of Toronto Press, 1977, p. 389.

15     John Murphy, *Imagining the Fifties: Private Sentiment and Political Culture in Menzies' Australia*, UNSW Press, Sydney, 2000, Chapter 8.

15     Home ownership rates: Jim Kemeny, *The Great Australian Nightmare: A Critique of the Home Ownership Ideology*, Georgian House, Melbourne, 1983, pp. 8–9. Figures based on calculations from the National Census.

15     94 per cent of the houses: Graeme Davison and Tony Dingle, Introduction, *The Cream Brick Frontier: Histories of Australian Suburbia*, Monash Publications in History, no. 19, 1995, p. 12.

15     Left interpretations: see Kemeny, *The Great Australian Nightmare*.

16     Addressing the voters in 1955: "The Ming Dynasty", *Hindsight*, ABC, 1990.

16     Donald Horne, *The Lucky Country: Australia in the Sixties*, classic edition, Angus & Robertson, Sydney, 1978, pp. 179–80.

18     Small-l liberal position: see Donald Horne, *Time of Hope: Australia 1966–72*, Angus & Robertson, Sydney, 1980, p. 15.

19     Fraser never managed to convince them otherwise: Philip Ayres, *Malcolm Fraser: A Biography*, William Heinemann, Melbourne, 1987, pp. 353, 430.

21–22   Howards's stance and its effect on his leadership: see Paul Kelly, *The End of Certainty: Power, Politics and Business in Australia*, Allen & Unwin, Sydney, pp. 420–28.

23     Howard: "The Role of Government: A Modern Liberal Approach", Menzies Research Centre 1995 National Lecture Series, 6 June 1995.

23–24   Left commentators on Howard: see for example Marian Sawer, "Populism and Public Choice in Australia and Canada: Turning Equality-seekers into 'Special interests'", and Carol Johnson, "Anti-Elitist Discourse in Australia: Intentional Influences and Comparisons", in Marian Sawer and Barry Hindess (eds), *Us and Them: Anti-Elitism in Australia*, API Network, Australia Research Institute, Curtin University of Technology, Perth, 2004.

25     *Future Directions: It's a Time for Plain Thinking*, Liberal and National Parties, December 1988. For more extended discussion, see Judith Brett, "Future Directions: New Conservatism's Manifesto", *Current Affairs Bulletin*, 96 (June 1989), pp. 11–17. Also, see Paul Kelly, *The End of Certainty*, Allen & Unwin, St Leonards, 1992, pp. 428–33.

25     *Future Directions* launch: *Sydney Morning Herald*, 5 December 1988.

25     "Building One Australia": *Future Directions*, p. 96.

27     Discussion focused on race: see Andrew Markus, *Race: John Howard and the remaking of Australia*, Allen & Unwin, Sydney, 2001.

27   "As with other disadvantaged Australians": *Future Directions*, p. 96.

28   He announced a review: doorstop interview, Wadeye Northern Territory, 6 April 2005, <www.pm.gov.au/news/interviews/Interview1395.html>.

28   "It is an absurd proposition": John Howard, "Treaty is a recipe for separatism", in K. Baker (ed.), *A Treaty with the Aborigines*, Institute for Public Affairs, Policy Issue no. 7, 1988, pp. 6–7.

29   Pamela Williams, *The Victory*, Allen & Unwin, St Leonards, 1997.

29   "Don't any of you ever be lectured": *The Victory*, p. 253.

30   Media transcript of address to the Queensland Division of the Liberal Party State Council, 22 September 1996, p. 4.

30   Andrew Robb, "The Liberal Campaign" in Clive Bean, Marian Simms, Scott Bennett & John Warhurst (eds), *The Politics of Retribution: The 1996 Federal Election*, Allen & Unwin, St Leonards, 1997, pp. 36–7.

31   Noel Pearson, address to Sydney Institute during 1996 election campaign, *The Sydney Papers*, Autumn 1996, vol. 8, no. 2.

31   Philip Ruddock on *The 7.30 Report*, ABC, 14 August 2001.

32–33   John Howard, Address to Australia Day Council's Australia Day Luncheon, Darling Harbour, Sydney, 24 January 1997, <http:/www.nla.gov.au/pmc/pressrel/ausday.html>.

33   "Our society is underpinned": Address to Federation of Ethnic Communities Council National Conference, Brisbane, 20 November 1998.

34   "Being Australian means": Keynote Address to Australian Council of Social Services National Congress, Adelaide, 5 November 1998.

34   "Being Australian embodies": "The Australia I Know" in Constitutional Essays on website of Australians for a Constitutional Monarchy, 11 November 2002.

34   "The open and unpretentious character": New Year's Message, 31 December 1999.

34   "When the self-esteem": "Peerless Bradman an inspiration across time", *Age*, 27 February 2001.

34   "In our highest aspirations": Fifth Annual Sir Edward "Weary" Dunlop Asialink Lecture, Melbourne, 11 November 1997.

34   "In only a few short weeks": Address to the Melbourne Press Club, 22 November 2000.

35   Russel Ward, *The Australian Legend*, Oxford University Press, Melbourne, 1958. See Michael Roe's excellent discussion of Ward's thesis and the responses to it in G.B. Davey and G. Seal, *The Oxford Companion to Australian Folklore*, Oxford University Press, Melbourne, 1993, pp. 34–41.

35    Conservative people have their own version: John Hirst, "The Pioneer Legend", *Historical Studies*, 18 (1978), pp. 316–37.

36    Tim Phillips and Philip Smith, "What is 'Australian'? Knowledge and Attitudes Among a Gallery of Contemporary Australians", *Australian Journal of Political Science*, July 2000, 35, 2, pp. 203–24.

36    John Hirst, *Australia's Democracy: A Short History*, Allen & Unwin, Sydney, 2002, p. 303.

37    Gerard Henderson, *A Howard Government? Inside the Coalition*, HarperCollins, Sydney, 1995, p. 27.

38    John Howard, Foreword, *Multicultural Australia: United in Diversity*, Department of Immigration, Multicultural and Indigenous Affairs, Canberra, 2003, p. 33.

38–39  Mark McKenna, "Howard's Warriors", in Raimond Gaita (ed.), *Why the War Was Wrong*, Text Publishing, Melbourne, 2003.

39    Benedict Anderson, *Imagined Communities: Reflections on the Origins and Spread of Nationalism*, Verso, London, 1983, p. 131.

41    Don Watson, in his *Recollections of a Bleeding Heart*, Knopf, Milsons Point, 2002, shows that Keating was prone to depression.

41–42  As some commentators have suggested: see David Adams, "John Howard as Prime Minister: The Enigma Variations" in Chris Aulich and Roger Wettenhall, *Howard's Second and Third Government: Australia Commonwealth Administration, 1998–2004*, UNSW Press, Sydney, 2005, p. 243.

43    David Marr, *Sydney Morning Herald*, 7 July 1989, cited by Mark McKenna in "Howard's Warriors".

44    A short account of the *Tampa* crisis can be found in Robert Manne (ed.), *The Howard Years*, pp. 36–9; a book-length account in David Marr and Marion Wilkinson, *Dark Victory*, Allen & Unwin, Sydney, 2003.

45    No one took responsibility: see Patrick Weller, *Don't Tell the Prime Minister*, Scribe, Carlton, 2002.

46    Harry Evans, "Executive and Parliament", in Chris Aulich and Roger Wettenhall, *Howard's Second and Third Governments*, pp. 46–7.

48    Howard addressed the National Reconciliation Planning Workshop, held at Old Parliament House, on 30 May 2005.

48    Mary Kalantzis, "Australia Fair: Realities and Banalities in the Howard Era", *Overland*, 178, 2005, pp. 12–16.

51    *The Woman*, 1 March 1930, p. 3.

51    Harold Holt, 'The Political Situation', 4 Feb 1957, cited in Ian Hancock, *National and Permanent?*, Melbourne University Press, Carlton, 2000, p. 169.

51–53  Don Aitkin, *Stability and Change in Australian Politics*, Australian National University

Press, Canberra, 1977. A second, revised edition, with findings from a second national survey conducted in the late 1970s was published in 1982 by Australian National University Press.

52    1996 figures from Ian McAllister, "Political Behaviour", in Dennis Woodward, Andrew Parkin and John Summers, *Government, Politics, Power and Policy in Australia*, 6th edition, Longman Cheshire, Melbourne, 1997, p. 251.

52    More aware, but also more pessimistic: Aitkin, 2nd edition, pp. 271–82.

53    The sharp slump seems to have occurred: McAllister, p. 251, Table 13.4. In 1987 a group of ANU-based political scientists began the Australian Electoral Study, based on a mail-back questionnaire distributed at this and every subsequent federal election.

53    The combined primary vote: Haydon Manning, "Voting Behaviour", in John Summers, Dennis Woodward and Andrew Parkin, *Government, Politics, Power and Policy in Australia*, 7th edition, Longman, Melbourne, 2002, p. 271.

53    So too were other factors: see in particular Hugh McKay, *Reinventing Australia: Australian Attitudes in the '90s*, Angus & Robertson, Sydney, 1993.

54    I have taken this typology of voters from Rodney Smith, *Australian Political Culture*, Pearson Education, Frenchs Forest, 2001, pp. 63–70.

58    Graeme Davison with Sheryl Yelland, *Car Wars*, Allen & Unwin, Crows Nest, 2004, pp. 112–116.

Guy Rundle

In a world where kids are routinely dosed with amphetamine variants to change their behaviour, and thousands upon thousands of people are persuaded that their misery is a "disease" unrelated to their lives or the society they live in, Gail Bell's essay is a fantastic demolition job – and all the more powerful for the manner in which it combines front-line experience with reflection and scholarship.

As I read it, Bell's argument is that the key causes of the whirlwind of anti-depressant prescription are to be found in a range of commercial and ideological practices. Bell describes how Merck fashioned the idea of undetected depression around its first antidepressant drug in the 1950s, to create an illness (and has continued doing so ever since). The tricylics became staples of GP-prescribing in the '60s and '70s at the same time as a culture of individualism and personal fulfilment developed – thus the second major cause became the widespread belief that one had a "right to be happy". As neurology developed and SSRIs entered the market, the markers and understanding of self as depressed (rather than "miserable" or "blue") became widespread, and people began presenting to GPs with implicit and explicit demands for drugs. GPs, by now overwhelmed with such patients and with limited capacity to offer counselling or referral, became increasingly likely to resort to prescribing such drugs – even when they knew that the cause of such moods was probably transient emotional exhaustion. Eventually they too, and pharmacists like Bell herself, found their thinking colonised by the physicalist model implied by the drug companies – depression was overwhelmingly a product of a neurochemical imbalance.

Bell is not an anti-psychiatrist in the manner of Szasz, nor is she a stiff upper lip depression-denialist. But my impression is that that she believes that the modern condition of depression is overwhelmingly a constructed one – made by corporations and then patients out of a mix of the raw materials of eternal conditions such as melancholia. Antidepressants have a place, because we would not want to deny people the free choice to use whatever works, but it would be better if people could pursue the cures offered by someone such as Burton in the *Anatomy of Melancholy* – living well, taking care of ourselves with food, wine, sleep, friends.

In arguing that a lot of what is self-labelled depression can be treated by living better, slowing down and other non-prescription pursuits, Bell has my complete agreement. Nevertheless, in diagnosing the causes of the antidepressant phenomenon I think Bell has missed a whole level of social life and social process, and that the absence of such an account makes it impossible for her to formulate a decisive answer to the question posed by "Angie", the troubled, Zoloft-taking, Foucault-reading 22-year-old whose encounter with Bell at a party provides the kick-off point for the essay. At the conclusion, Bell can only say in response to Angie's existential concerns about taking such drugs, that sometimes we need to do so – a non-conclusion that indicates that the essay has not got at the key questions about depression and drugs.

Let me suggest an alternative interpretation of the current spread of the depression diagnosis. Much of what is currently called "depression" is a new and real social-psychological disorder, produced by widespread transformations of Western societies in the past three decades. In response to these transformations – in shorthand, the media revolution, and the changes to work and home life, and social space and culture – many of us have become more vulnerable to the onset of feelings that selfhood, existence and connection to others have been pulverised, and that meaning and contentment are not only absent, but impossible. Depression and melancholia have existed throughout modernity and before, but a widespread low-grade depression has now become an existential common cold. Yet it is not simply an ennui – it is a more deeply rooted state that differs from a condition such as "the blues". In some cases (but only some) it produces a real neurochemical change in the subject. In many others it simply produces a view of self as hopelessly miserable – but many such people often latch onto a neurochemical explanation because it offers a simple, quick and physicalised explanation for what would otherwise be interpreted as social failure.

Depression, as an experience and as a social object, is separated from misery by its categorical nature. The depressive cannot remember the feeling of being cheerful or purposeful, cannot imagine the circumstances by which one would become so, or by which one would feel connected to another human being, and so on. Everything has slipped through the floorboards – the world (in the sense of a meaningful place, a field of purpose), the self (in the form of a loss of desire) and others (the internalised presence of loved ones). This is more or less a cultural universal – almost every culture has a term for "sadness without object or without end".

Yet such experiences are much rarer in traditional cultures, and even in more closely knit and stable modern cultures, than in our own. Why would this be? My suggestion is that in many lives, we see a comparative absence of the structures that shape a stable, meaningful existence. Even a few decades ago, most people lived within much closer networks of kin and neighbourhood. Obviously this was often constricting and frustrating, but it was also the guarantor of a certain sense of real identity, grouped around extended family, clan, neighbourhood, congregation, union, association, whatever. The identity of being X's son, daughter, wife, husband, a fitter and turner, a Methodist of St Mark's parish, etc., was, in other words, both internal and external. Not only was one connected to others, one was recognised and known by them – and they by you. A certain minimum, rock-solid selfhood was guaranteed by these relationships, as was a world of relatively stable meaning, mediated by symbols and ceremonies, ethnic, religious, national or otherwise.

Of course such a world was often prejudiced and stifling, a point to which I'll return. But a solid and meaningful existence was, in effect, a firebreak on sadness. Because one's worth and self were not dependent on a self-made trajectory of success, career, power and the like, there was less capacity for bad events and disappointments to become all-consuming annihilations, negations of self.

In the past few decades we have swept those social networks away as comprehensively as we have many of the physical neighbourhoods they dwelt in. Much of this has had a positive dimension – people get an education, mobility, travel, befriend and marry outside their ethnicity and so on. But such a world places an extraordinary burden on the individual, since they must increasingly make their own networks and worlds of meaning. Recognition – the sense that we are known and of worth to others – must be earned, and that raises the possibility that we will fail to earn it, *and that that failure will be unmitigated*. At the same time as this is going on, economic changes – the demolition of the manufacturing base in particular – have reduced the number of places where people can find permanent work and stable workplaces. As the mediating institutions fall away, the individual finds that there is nothing between them and the entire world – now coming in their headset/console as a plethora of images of, increasingly, power, wealth and celebrity. Such images increasingly become the "others" that people – especially adolescents – internalise. By definition they cannot provide a stable world of meaning, nor can they offer reciprocal recognition.

The result is a society whose principal purpose, it can seem, is to make as many people as possible feel like shit as often as possible. All the time. When people have felt like shit for long enough, they go to their GP. By this time they have felt like shit for so long that the psychological factors may – in some cases – have caused physiological changes. When the prescribed antidepressants kick in – in the second to third week of regular use (serotonin levels are elevated immediately by SSRIs, but it takes weeks for knock-on processes, such as re-regulation of cortisol levels, to occur) – the depressed person feels a basic sense of life they had forgotten was possible – the sensuous particularity of the world, and desire within it. Others benefit from the social effect of being medicated: the pill gives hope, evidence of care by another, absolution from failure and the renewed sense of specialness ("I'm a depressive!") necessary to a functioning ego.

The question is this: have we created a society in which large numbers of people – even when they are in society – do not really feel of it? In the midst of cities, jobs, study, they are more exposed to bad times that can readily tumble into a permanent sense of malaise and reduced energy. We have assumed that human nature, being transformable, is infinitely so – that there is no social-psychological cost to living in a hi-tech, high-mobility world. If antidepressants have any effect above that of a placebo (and we may eventually find that they don't), it is because we are "hard-wired" for a form of social life which involves reciprocity and mutual recognition, and the prolonged absence of that will have a neurochemical effect.

If that is the case, then antidepressant medication is not properly understood as a treatment for a disease. Rather it is a crude chemical biotechnology designed to re-engineer humans in line with the needs of a global market society. This may explain the paradoxical side effects of "happy pills" – the creation of anxiety and suicidality. Since the physical is only one level of the psychological make-up of a human being, the energy inserted at the physical level can come into conflict with an untransformed unhappiness felt at the level of self. The antidepressants may give people either the energy to feel shriekingly, energetically alarmed about their distress (anxiety) or the strength to do something once and for all about the fact that they still feel worthless, futile and alone.

If that is the case – and such an argument builds on the insights of a whole tradition of social commentary by writers such as Riesman, Sennett, Fromm and writers from the *Arena* group – then Bell, with the best of motives, has misread the social process that is occurring, and placed too much emphasis on the surface ideological effects of the Prozac revolution – the profit-driven nature of Big

Pharma, the mechanistic understanding of the human being advanced by many GPs and psychiatrists. Hence she is at an impasse when confronted with someone who both feels better because of the drugs, but guilty or worried at the undermining of authenticity created by them. The cultural problem is not that SSRIs don't work, but that they do.

For many GPs and health professionals, however, there is no problem. They have identified an effective remedy for contemporary problems – certainly one that is more effective than either the "stiff upper lip" school, various forms of psychotherapy, or the idea of living well.

However, the problem is that the widespread use of such medicines undermines the cultural framework – the network of social meaning – that it seeks to reintroduce its users to. Like it or not, SSRIs transform the emotional meaning of life events. They're not tranquilisers – they don't even things out to blandness – but they do provide a certain level of chemically supplied enthusiasm which would not otherwise be there. If one person within a group is thus reconstituted, it is of no great import. But what if two are? What is the status of a conversation between two chemically altered subjects? Or a whole group of people? And what happens if successive generations of these drugs become more effective at s(t)imulating certain types of emotional response?

It should be clear that at some point in that scenario the meaning of social life drains away. If I can never know whether the laugh or the smile of the other is because of their relationship to me and the meaning of what I have said to them, or whether it is because molecule BX11185G is playing on receptor site DC9122Z, and if they cannot know the same about me, then what is the meaning of our exchange, or our relationship? Once the chemical transformation of emotional life crosses a certain threshold, then that question becomes a central one. The result eventually is a collapse of trust, connection and meaning. Eventually the chemical stimulation of emotion would cease to work, because the emotional webs it sought to counterfeit were no longer there.

Take, by way of example, the figure of Angie, whom Bell introduced. She is not-untypical – humanities-educated, ambitious to take a place in the cosmopolitan global world, eager for an experience of depth (else why would she study philosophers and theorists), yet seemingly crushed by both some violence in her past and a sense of the world's indifference ("I'm not going to commit suicide. I haven't made my mark on the world"). Zoloft enables her – or she believes it does – to acquire some of the personality traits necessary to making her mark – a degree of energy and confidence which will get her to New York, where she "falls in love with a skyline". When she gets there, like as not, she'll meet people very much like her – on or off various combinations and versions of antidepressants and anti-anxiolitics. What is going on when a bunch of people from around the world are having a conversation, and they're all on an antidepressant? Is anything happening at all? Or, in the pursuit of difference has she simply encountered a mass-produced sameness? In looking for an experience of depth has she come into a more superficial experience? The journey to New York was – as all such journeys are – not just about what one sees, but about what one becomes, about individuation. Yet if the prerequisite for "becoming" is to use a chemical to bypass some of one's fears and anxieties, what has one become? And once again, if that can be got away with on an individual basis, what happens to the meaning of experience when a significant number of people are doing it?

Such concerns are usually labelled as science-fictive by the enthusiasts for chemical alteration. Taken in isolation, they are. A range of new miracle pills are, of themselves, not going to turn us into autonomous emotional zombies. However, there are two key qualifications to make about that. The first is that, in areas of social life where antidepressant use has become so widespread as to be dominant, it has, I believe, contributed to a cultural change – in particular, to a higher degree of atomisation and emotional solipsism. There are other factors in this, but mood control pills contribute to a wilful dissociation from social life – from seeing what one is as connected to what one does, or is a part of. The second caveat is that the current generation of pills are so crude in effect that they do not, of themselves, have the capacity to more exactly reprogram the brain. But with the rise of genetic medicine (as Bell notes) future generations of drugs may allow for a much greater hi-tech manipulation of one's emotional states. Whether or not that sounds like something from a Philip K. Dick novel, it is worth starting to think about what sort of effect it would have on a culture.

What many people want to avoid by using antidepressants is the process of reflection and rethinking by which one's fears and dark areas are reclaimed, and by which authentic relations with others are built. And who can blame them? Our culture – especially in the last five to ten years – has become one in which strength, aggressiveness, selfishness and hardness have become the cardinal virtues. The hard-bodied ethos of the gym, the competitive nature of contractual and outsourced work, the visibility of enormous wealth, the surgically enhanced standards of beauty, and the theme of social-life-as-competition (à la Big Brother) have become central motifs. Even in areas of public emotional life – pop music, TV shows like Oprah – the "touchy-feely" content is frequently subsumed under the idea of shaping oneself for maximum success. Part of this is an inheritance of the individualistic strands of the '60s and '70s (the "me" decade), but these ideas have been substantially transformed – the introspective and pastoral dimension of the "me" decade has been discarded (thus Angie rejects psychotherapy by describing it as "live your dream"-style blather) and the individual self-shaping has been fused with the cultural and economic imperatives of neo-liberalism. This is one step on from "greed is good" – it is not money per se, but power, recognition and the capacity to "make a mark" that one shapes oneself towards. What could be more self-defeating than to detour via the introspection and self-disassembling of therapy? What could be worse than to admit that something is wrong?

So where does that leave us? On the basis that the indefinitely expanding use of mood-modifying drugs is culturally contradictory, we can suggest an ethos for chemical therapies that gives one something more to say than Bell's comment that a younger generation finds the contradictions easier to live with. We could say, for example, that in most (but not all) cases one should try to avoid chemical antidepressants until one has thoroughly explored the reasons for the feeling – with or without some form of guided psychotherapy. There is something inherently pointless about making such pills one's first (or second) resort if one's aim is to explore the deep experiences of life that might be offered by the writings of Foucault or a city such as New York.

At the same time we can say that there is a chemical dimension to our emotional lives, and that chemical solutions are much better as a later, or last, resort than as an earlier one. An extreme humanist response – never use antidepressants – is silly and futile, given what we know about the relationship between self and brain. And there are cases – people with a family history of bipolar disorder (manic depression), for example – where it is reasonable to try chemical solutions much earlier, because the condition itself can be reasonably supposed to be genetic in origin, and part of a relatively autonomous neurological process. It is also possible (though more hypothetical) that victims of sustained violent child sexual abuse have been "neurologically scarred" by traumatic events that occurred at a time when the brain was still in development and that some – but not all – such people may require some mood stabilisation prior to trying to work through problems and issues at the psychological level. The point is that all such suggestions – tentative and exploratory as they must be – are a product of our developing understanding of the self–brain relationship. Rather than throwing up our hands and treating these as insoluble contradictions, or thinking wishfully about a pre-scientific world of "melancholia", we have to take the opportunity science offers to come to a fuller understanding of what it is to be human, and build a relatively complex ethos of psychiatry on its foundations.

Of course this will often fall on deaf ears. You only live once, and many people feel an urgent existential demand to "get a life". Who wants to be told that they should try to work and think through their problems? Even the argument for psychotherapy is of limited use since some forms of it – psychoanalysis, for example – take people further in the direction of individualising a cultural problem, rather than out towards the world. Psychotherapy – and more general sources of social understanding, such as high-school level social studies – should incorporate a more critical social dimension which helps people to understand the rapid manner in which everyday life is being transformed, and the degree to which issues of power, media and community have a role in forming selfhood. The current depression "epidemic" is a social symptom of a wider cultural problem, rather than a particular effect of more superficial commercial practices and ideologies.

Guy Rundle

Gordon Parker

Gail Bell writes evocatively and well. Worryingly well. As an "opinion piece"
her essay advances valid concerns about the current use and application of antidepressant drugs in our society. But it is also an "edgy" essay and the edginess
makes it difficult to make this a frisson-free response. Let's look at the essayist's
style before addressing issues of substance, for the question is whether such
polemic dressed in the cloak of reason leads to unbalanced conclusions.

Bell's essay starts with a vignette of Angie. It is an amorphous vignette, so we
do not know whether Angie has a primary mood disorder, another psychiatric
condition, is suffering from a mix of illicit and prescribed medication, is experiencing a side effect of prescribed medication or is merely "overwrought". In
the absence of such information, any response by a health professional to the
question of whether she should stay on antidepressant medication is straight-
forward. But Bell's own interpretation of her response is telling – she says she
provides "the tame dove answers of my white-coat training". Commonsense and
prudence alone would suggest that she encourage Angie to be reviewed by her
health practitioner – as she did – but Bell's "tame dove" reference suggests, also,
a frustration with an assumed health hierarchy and a wider dissatisfaction with
the management of depression by health professionals. While health professionals can defend themselves against her anti-allopathic rhetoric, the harm lies in
the fact that many depressed patients will be unsettled by her essay.

While I share some of Bell's concerns, I would like to offer another perspective on several issues. First, some history. As Bell notes, there has been a
longstanding division of depressive disorders into two principal "types". The
first, once called "endogenous depression", now "melancholic depression", is
the quintessentially biological type, with a strong genetic contribution, underpinned by a number of derangements in biological functioning and having
some stereotypical features. While minimally responsive to placebo and talking

therapies (psychotherapy and counselling), it is highly responsive to physical treatments, including antidepressant drugs.

The second type, once variably called "exogenous", "neurotic" or "reactive", was more likely to be brought on by the impact of a stressful life event perturbing an individual with certain vulnerability factors (e.g. personality style), and therefore was best addressed by psychotherapeutic strategies.

This simple binary model – for both modelling and treating depressive conditions – made decisions about antidepressant drug therapy relatively simple. Argued since biblical times, it held sway until the middle of the twentieth century, but lost currency as a consequence of several key changes that, in turn, progressively clouded our capacity to understand "depression".

The first antidepressant drug (the tricyclic drug Imipramine) was "discovered" a little more than fifty years ago. The manufacturers, Ciba-Geigy, did not wish to take that drug to market as their analyses indicated that there were insufficient depressed people in the world for the drug to return a profit, and it was only after strong protest advocacy in the United States (by consumers) that it was released. When we consider the sales of antidepressants over the last decade, that judgment by Ciba-Geigy may seem inexplicable. But "depression" in the middle of the twentieth century essentially comprised severe expressions of "biological depression" (psychotic or melancholic depression) that resulted in a percentage of people being hospitalised, generally in asylums as few general hospital psychiatry units existed. Such connotations meant that "depression" joined with other severe mental illnesses in being stigmatised, discouraging the many with "less severe" expressions from attending health practitioners. Diagnosis and detection were therefore limited.

Now, for the first time, there were drugs that were strikingly effective in assisting those with melancholic depression. And in medicine, when any therapy is discovered to be useful for a target condition, there is a rapid move to test its efficacy beyond its initial boundaries. Such diffusion compromises clarity, even when the "disease" model is well-defined, but in this case the phenomenon was also wedded to a new "muddy" definition of depression.

The template for modelling and treating "depression" was radically changed by the introduction of a North American model for categorising psychiatric disorders. The Diagnostic and Statistical Manual of Mental Disorders – Third Edition (DSM-III) was published in 1980 by the American Psychiatric Association. In the preceding decade, senior American academic psychiatrists had become increasingly concerned about the psychoanalytic emphasis in North American theorising and practice. They could see psychiatry losing its roots in medicine and risking irrelevance. They sought to bring psychiatry back into medicine by emphasising psychiatry's biological focus and instituting a strong scientific approach. DSM-III categorisation involved "structured criteria" for disorders (to ensure scientific reliability) but unfortunately ignored any consideration of cause or aetiology.

The DSM-III model characterised depression as a single disorder that varied in severity, duration and persistence. It was a model that described a unitary concept with various "dimensions", and therefore introduced pseudo-categories of "major depression" and "minor depression". Yet while the diagnosis of "major depression" has gravitas, in reality it is non-specific – a "muddy" definition. An individual is required to have a significantly depressed mood for at least two weeks, have some degree of impairment, and several symptoms such as appetite or sleep disturbance, loss of energy and loss of interest and pleasure in usual activities. While the DSM-III description of a characteristic "major depressive episode" largely captures the severe biological melancholic depressive disorders, the clinical criteria listed for "major depression" were structured according to one of the guiding principles of DSM-III – to have such criteria "describe the lowest order of inference necessary to describe the characteristic features of the disorder". Thus, while an individual with melancholic depression might experience such profound and pathological guilt that they feel it their duty to kill themselves, the relevant DSM-III "guilt" criterion now allowed "thin" symptoms such as "feelings of worthlessness and self-reproach" to build to a new definition of "depression".

Thus, after 1980 "clinical depression" was re-defined, with the "bar" for meeting a diagnosis set low, resulting in many more people with varying levels of depression being diagnosed as a "clinical case". "Depression" moved from (predominantly) "disease" status to encompass a range of conditions: diseases, disorders, syndromes, predicaments and possibly extensions of normal mood states – although the "new" definition tended to position all such "conditions" as "disease" states.

The redefinition of clinical depression not only led to much higher diagnosed prevalence rates of current and lifetime depression, but now the majority of identified sufferers had the "less severe" non-melancholic or "atypical" expressions, where the role of the tricyclic antidepressants had been shown to be less useful.

The homogenising DSM-III model had a powerful effect on the approach to treatment. Rather than progressively develop a matrix where identified depressive types were married with preferential specific drug and non-drug treatment strategies, an "integrative" movement occurred. "Integrative" theories conceded that clinical depression could be caused by many factors (e.g. genetic, developmental, psychosocial), but these individual nuances could be ignored as they were all channelled along a "final common pathway" to create "major depression" – a muddily defined pseudo-entity that has become entrenched, homogenising multiple expressions of depression, irrespective of their biological, psychological or social cause.

Predictably, subsequent research into this "entity" has failed to identify consistent causes. Perhaps more importantly, when quite different treatments for "major depression" are compared in randomised controlled trials, all appear comparable in their efficacy. Thus, antidepressants of differing classes tend not to differ from each other or from the major psychotherapies or even from "natural" remedies, such as St John's Wort, in their efficacy.

We should not be surprised by such an opaque result. Test a treatment non-specifically (i.e. as a universal treatment, relevant across the board) for a non-specific pseudo-entity like major depression, and we should anticipate a non-specific result, with all treatments given a guernsey. In essence, the dodo bird verdict: "All have won and all must have prizes."

Another effect was the emergence of contending colonisers, each seeking to occupy the new territorial map, and each offering a simple view of the muddy landscape. The majority view (reflecting the "new biological psychiatry" and the influence of the pharmaceutical industry) now interprets major depression as a biological condition reflecting a "chemical imbalance" quite independent of personality, and requiring correction of the perturbed neurotransmitter circuits by the prescription of an antidepressant drug. A contending view comes from psychologists who argue that major depression is the consequence of a faulty "attribution style", and requires cognitive behaviour therapy. And other professionals put forward their own singular treatment modality as the best means of treating "it".

In essence, a procrustean model has developed whereby the individual's condition is fitted to the therapist's discipline or training rather than the therapy being "fitted" to the characteristics of the individual's disorder. This is quite at variance with the standard medical model and of great concern. Imagine if you had clinically significant breathlessness ("major breathlessness"). You would not expect a general practitioner to prescribe a treatment merely on the basis of that non-specific diagnosis only. You would expect your health practitioner to identify the cause (e.g. asthma, pneumonia or a pulmonary embolus) and then rationally derive a cause-weighted treatment.

It is held that destigmatising depression (a process which has been extremely successful) requires a simple definition. Characterising depression as an "it", and encouraging recourse to diagnosis and treatment, is the message that dominates most campaigns. Unfortunately, many health professionals have also adopted a simplistic and erroneous model, one that compromises treatment for many sufferers. It seems to us – at the Black Dog Institute – that it is just as easy to communicate a more realistic "horses for courses" model (i.e. that there are many types of depression, some which respond best to medication, others to certain specific psychotherapies, others to support and counselling). We argue that health professionals should seek to establish and disseminate diagnostic and treatment matrices, as are produced in other areas of medicine (e.g. best treatments for differing cancers, for managing differing types of diabetes).

The redefinition of "depression" to include a majority of non-melancholic conditions coincided with the introduction of the narrow-action SSRI antidepressant drugs – and with many sufferers of these "less biological" depressive disorders finding them beneficial. For the first time in my professional career as a psychiatrist, I encountered patients (and people at social gatherings) talking comfortably about how an SSRI antidepressant had aborted their depression and allowed them to function again. Most had a non-melancholic depressive disorder. The benefits of SSRIs stemmed not only from an antidepressant action but also from an apparent capacity to mute emotional dysregulation and worrying, modifying the response to stress and assisting many out of depression, as well as decreasing the chance of recurrence. It was clear that the new SSRI antidepressants were of benefit for a percentage of people with depressive conditions who – previously reluctant to seek help because of stigma – had suffered in silence and in depression-induced darkness.

Because many of these people appear to be functioning well, they risk invoking the "they should pull their socks up instead of taking medication" response. But we have all seen people with medical conditions (e.g. diabetes, blood pressure, cancer) who appear to be functioning well. Do we challenge their right to take medication and diminish them with *ad hominem* statements inferring self-indulgence or "spinelessness"? It is on this issue that I part company with Bell, for her views risk activating such responses.

Clearly, the SSRIs were promoted over-enthusiastically by the pharmaceutical companies and by many health professionals. While their side-effect profile is only marginally superior to that of the older antidepressants, we initially misjudged the reality that, like most medications, they do have a number of significant side effects for a percentage of people, and can be less effective than the older broad-action antidepressants for managing the melancholic depressive disorders. Nevertheless, a confluence of factors had set the scene.

"Depression" as redefined had a much higher prevalence than had been previously quantified; its non-specific definition allowed the new antidepressant drugs to be positioned as a universal ("one-size-fits-all") therapy; and drug therapy was cheaper and easier to roll out than psychotherapy. This model also delivered a much broader market to the pharmaceutical industry. And finally, sufferers of a "chemical imbalance" were not blamed for it, nor did they need to contribute to making a recovery from their depression.

As with the take-up of any effective drug (in any area of medicine), excessive enthusiasm has tempered over time. Steroids are another example of this. Initially perceived as wonder drugs, their extremely troubling side effects for a percentage of people were progressively identified and they were also found to be less effective than first judged. The same phenomenon has occurred with the newer antidepressants, with all the passion of a new relationship and its course reflected in the literature. Kramer's book Listening to Prozac captured the proselytising evangelical infatuation stage, echoed in initial media reports. Later, the media became less endeared with the SSRIs (a "so what, everyone's on them" scenario), with Beyond Prozac and Prozac Nation capturing a drift from fidelity. And in recent times, the backlash evidences a falling out of love, with stories emphasising the side effects of the SSRIs, criticising the pharmaceutical industry and sensationalising any real risk of SSRI-induced suicidality – as captured in the book Let Them Eat Prozac. "Divorce" is now in the offing ... some antidepressants risk being withdrawn from market or having their prescription markedly curtailed.

It is human nature to respond in anger when we have invested our faith in something and been disappointed when it falls short. The story is a regrettably common one in medicine (e.g. L-Dopa for Parkinson's Disease; HRT treatment) and therefore not unique to psychiatry. The risk is in throwing the baby out with the bath water.

How to proceed when there is a dumb model for the depressive disorders out there, which homogenises multiple depressive types to "depression as an 'it'", which ignores cause, and which encourages a view that treatments are universally relevant? In such circumstances, it must be expected that some individuals will be "under-treated" (e.g. those with a melancholic disorder who fail to receive a physical treatment) and others effectively "over-treated" (e.g. those who neither need nor respond to an antidepressant drug, and who receive a seemingly endless parade of drug therapies). Mismanagement of depression occurs as much from errors of omission (e.g. a therapist giving meandering chicken-soup advice to a sufferer month after month) as from commission (e.g. excessive reliance on medication), and it is the paradigm failures across the board – not just those associated with antidepressant medication – that need to be identified and addressed. As noted earlier, I argue for more horse sense – respecting sub-typing and differential treatment recommendations, a "horses for courses" paradigm that allows situations when an antidepressant (and the right one) is necessary and sufficient, when it is best viewed as an adjunct, and when it is irrelevant or inappropriate.

Now, to return to Bell's key points. Firstly, she is concerned about "the stratospheric increase in antidepressant prescribing". This disquiet about increased prescribing of a drug, echoed by many journalists, is rarely expressed in the non-psychiatric domain of medicine – and often has stigmatising undertones. If not a cost issue, the salient parameters should be utilitarian ones at the community level (is the expansion in prescribing associated with more people being helped out of their mood state?) and cost-benefit ones at the individual level (if trialled on an antidepressant, does the individual – and their clinician – judge the benefits to outweigh the costs?).

My concern is with Bell's *ad hominem* "pull up your socks" stance towards many with depressive conditions. The title *The Worried Well* joins with a term that I have never previously heard – "misery-chic" – as misanthropic, trivialising and belittling. The risk to her assertions is that, in seeking to damn those engaging in cosmetic psychopharmacology, she unfairly demeans those with significant mood disorders. Such people already have enough of a struggle dealing with the black fog of their dis-ease, without having to doubt whether they now should continue with the medication that they had thought to be both valid and helpful.

Just as with the proverbial elephant in the room, the elephantine abstract concept of "major depression" tempts all of us to tunnel-vision – a monolithic understanding of depression and a for-or-against approach to antidepressant medication. In the same way that one might discuss footballers solely in terms of their athletic prowess, ignoring any antisocial behaviour, or vice versa, such one-eyed and stereotypical generalisations risk a lack of perspective. For some depression sufferers, antidepressant drugs are life-savers, for others life-enablers, for others of no use, and, for a percentage, a form of medication that makes things worse because of its irrelevance or side effects. The balance can be influenced by clinical sophistication in melding the art and the science. Clinicians who practise according to a sophisticated and richer model, who understand when to prescribe an antidepressant, who inform patients about salient side effects and provide pre-emptive strategies to reduce their chance or their effects, will continue to advance the management of depression. But, even in such optimal circumstances, our ability to successfully predict individual responses in advance remains unsatisfactory – but the same caveat applies to non-drug approaches to depression and to many non-psychiatric conditions.

Bell's polemic embodies the frustrations of the disappointed and the sceptical, and perhaps her own disappointment when an SSRI failed to meet her expectations. However, extrapolation of her inner world to a world view is of greater concern when it is wedded with an austere solution. Her essay finishes with a thought that is edgy at best but puritanical in its import. Bell ponders how realistic it is to turn back the clock to when treatments were simpler, non-drug based and "traditional" ("a good night's sleep and a bowel movement"). Medicine has allowed many choices (e.g. childbirth with anaesthesia vs natural childbirth) and we benefit from such advances. Extrapolating from romantic and simplistic visions of "the good old days" – which never were – risks shaming many into suffering in silence.

So, while I share many of Bell's concerns, she diminishes the fact that the depressive disorders are painful and disabling, and so distorts the meaning and value of her analysis. A lack of balance, chemical or otherwise, is, at the end of the day, a lack of balance.

Gordon Parker

Correspondence

## Elizabeth A. Wilson

"Worried well" is a term of disdain. It has become a common way of dismissing the distress experienced by a significant sector of the community, and it does little to help us understand what is at stake – politically and psychologically – in the current psychopharmaceutical climate. Much of the rhetorical strength of Gail Bell's analysis follows from the distinction she makes between the seriously depressed and those "with the sort of normal sadness that afflicts us all, the people with low-level sorrow". In the first group, Bell asks us to imagine a twenty-something woman who self-harms, or a withdrawn and suicidal teenager who doesn't leave his bed. These are the people for whom antidepressants were invented, Bell claims; and there is no question in her mind that these disabling conditions warrant pharmaceutical intervention. On the other hand, we have the worried well. These are the people who have fallen victim to less significant worries – falling out of love or becoming stressed at work. A psychiatrist might categorise these kinds of ills as dysthymia (chronic, low-level sadness). Bell is much less convinced that the worried well require the level of pharmaceutical treatment they have been receiving (mainly from GPs) since the introduction of Prozac in the late 1980s.

While the category of the worried well may be intuitively appealing, it is extraordinarily unhelpful for analysing the nature of depression and for thinking about its treatment. Distinctions between the deserving and undeserving depressed profoundly underestimate the psychological, and indeed physiological, issues at stake. That there are different kinds of depression is not in dispute. Depressions can be major, bipolar, post-natal, dysthymic, acute, seasonal, fatal. They can manifest with or without psychotic features, with or without the co-morbidity of trauma, an eating disorder, indefinite detention or cancer. Bell seems less interested in the heterogeneity of depressive experience than she is in demarcating a particular subgroup of depressives (the worried well), and then withdrawing empathy and the justification for pharmaceutical treatment from them.

Bell suggests that the phrase "worried well" comes from Freud. It does not. But what she may be thinking of is a widely circulated quote from Freud, in which he advises that the best psychoanalysis can do is to turn acute misery into everyday unhappiness. Let me quote Freud fully – as I think attention to the detail may enable us to find a way past Bell's rhetorical, political and (worst of all) moral demarcations. In 1895, at the very end of his *Studies on Hysteria*, Freud writes:

> When I have promised my patients help or improvement by means of a cathartic treatment [the precursor to psychoanalysis proper] I have often been faced by this objection: "Why, you tell me yourself that my illness is probably connected with my circumstances and the events of my life. You cannot alter these in any way. How do you propose to help me, then?" And I have been able to make this reply: "No doubt fate would find it easier than I do to relieve you of your illness. But you will be able to convince yourself that much will be gained if we succeed in transforming your hysterical misery into common unhappiness. With a mental life that has been restored to health you will be better armed against that unhappiness."

In these early years, when Freud was immersed in the treatment of hysteria, he was finely attuned to the needs of his patients. His texts, while fully medicalised, are notable for their empathic engagement with women in particular. He makes no judgment about whether or not a patient ought to be unwell. He treats every patient on her merits, and he asks us to take every affliction seriously, even those that seem petty, disagreeable or self-indulgent. Bell, in repeatedly making a distinction between those who are miserable and those who are merely unhappy, lacks this attentive eye for psychological detail. Where she is concerned that the category of depression has become too large as a result of the big pharma's marketing and advertising, I am troubled that the category of "common unhappiness" has been expanded so that increasing levels of stress, anger, low mood and self-hatred are seen as a normal part of life. In the end, the politics and rhetoric of those who agitate against the overuse of antidepressants often feel disdainful of certain kinds of emotional distress. Put simply, the category "worried well" tends to obstruct rather than facilitate an understanding of the experience of depression.

There is now a large body of evidence that suggests not only that drug treatments and psychological treatments of depression work best when combined, but that – more provocatively – psychological treatments have material effects on the nervous system. Freud's work was prescient in understanding this essential intimacy of neurology and words. The choice between Freud and Prozac (to use Bell's shorthand) turns out to be less ideologically and medically definitive than we have been led to believe in the post-war, post-Freudian, pro-pharmaceutical years of the twentieth century. Psychoanalysis and psychopharmacology are not competing ideologies of depressive malady – they are different lines of attack into the same bioaffective system. Which line of attack, for how long and at what level of intensity is an issue for each individual in consultation with their mental health practitioner and in accordance with that patient's circumstances, anxieties and emotional preferences. It is not an issue of principle or politics that can be adjudicated in advance (and for this reason it is exceedingly difficult for those not working at the psychological coalface to know whether or not antidepressants are being over-used). The pro-Freud/anti-Freud, pro-drug/anti-drug debates that have occupied the political field since the anti-psychiatry movement of the 1960s are becoming less potent as we see growing sophistication (and increasing collaboration) in psychodynamic and psychopharmaceutical research. In the years to come, the difference between treating a depression biochemically and treating it psychologically may be less fraught than we currently suppose. With this future in mind, Bell's call for a greater variety of resources for treating mild to moderate depression need not also be a battle cry against psychopharmaceuticals.

Perhaps most importantly of all, what Freud is advocating in his treatment of hysteria is not an acceptance of common unhappiness, but the building up of psychic robustness so that life's misfortunes and heartbreaks can be understood and worked through. This kind of robustness is precisely what depressives (major and minor) lack. Without this psychic strength, every blow – even the smallest – is amplified in force. The damage from being battered by the quotidian events of life ought not to be underestimated. For many, many patients, antidepressants have proven themselves to be an effective bulwark against such everyday battles. Freud himself struggled for the last decades of his life, without the aid of psychopharmaceuticals, to find his emotional equilibrium and buoyancy after the death of his favourite daughter and a grandchild, the exhausting effects of professional battles, the deprivations the Great War had inflicted on those living in Vienna, and then finally the onslaught of cancer. Readers of Bell's essay who are dissatisfied by her disregard for the harmful effects of mild depression may want to look at Peter Kramer's new book *Against Depression*. Kramer (the author of the 1993 bestseller *Listening to Prozac*) argues that chronic low-level depression eats away at us not just psychically, but also physiologically. Far from being benign, the dysthymic complaints of the worried well register a serious attrition of psyche and nerves. There are no gains to be made from moderate depression (as Bell contemplates), and no excuses for letting it proliferate among individuals or across the culture under the romantic ideal of artistic genius, comedic spark or existential rumination.

What we need in the public sphere is a greater empathy for what depression – even when minor – feels like, and a wider awareness of the damage it does to our emotional strength, our relationships, our bodies and our capacity to work and play. One of the things that chronic low-level depression may do is make those so afflicted unlikeable and tedious. Further distaste, elicited under the shaming rubric of the "worried well", only makes the political and emotional challenges of dealing with depression that much harder.

Elizabeth A. Wilson

Correspondence

# David Webb

In Gail Bell's essay, *The Worried Well*, I have been the suicidal "surly boy in the next street" that Bell assumes "is the patient for whom the mood-enhancing drugs were invented". Although her candid and thoughtful essay goes some way towards correcting the widespread misinformation about depression, her analysis does not quite go far enough and her own bio-reductionist bias is revealed in cases of so-called major depression.

Bell claims that "about 15 per cent of major depressions proceed to suicide," echoing another frequently heard assertion that depression is the major *cause* of suicide. One prominent suicide expert, Professor Robert Goldney from Adelaide University, uses a "real estate analogy" that the "most important contributing factors to suicidal behaviors are depression, depression, depression". All these assertions rest on the assumption that depression is a medical illness, an assumption that Bell correctly questions for the worried well but not for "major depression".

Bell reminds us that since the 1950s depression has been reconceptualised and "relabelled" as a disease, rather than a symptom, in order to "render it visible to medicine's gaze". Her essay exposes how big pharma was instrumental in this though she herself maintains the view that "depression is what depression has always been ... a cluster of symptoms." Indeed, the *Diagnostic and Statistical Manual of Mental Disorders*, the bible of modern psychiatric diagnosis, defines depression solely in terms of a cluster of symptoms. No aetiology, cause or explanation is offered, but this is sufficient for the American Psychiatric Association (the authors of the *DSM*) to declare depression a psychiatric disorder. With this "decree" from the APA, depression acquires the status of a "mental illness".

The phrase "mental illness" is a metaphor. It uses the language of biological medicine to describe and explore the psychological and emotional pain of mental suffering. But the mind is not a biological organ. There is no mind "thing" that can get ill in the way that a liver or a kidney can. To speak of mental illness is to speak metaphorically. Although the metaphor may be of use (though personally I think it's a weak one), it is a serious mistake when a metaphor is taken as a literal truth. This serious mistake, a category error that confuses the psychology of the mind with the biology of the brain, has in recent decades become the status quo in psychiatry and, in turn, in the general community. But the consequences of this selling of depression as a medical illness extends beyond the commercial excesses of big pharma.

A clear example from my own life story is that once I was diagnosed with major depression, this became the *explanation* for my suicidal feelings and behaviour, and antidepressants were prescribed. I tried a couple of different SSRI drugs and although I didn't have the nasty side effects that some people report (the commonly experienced "sexual dysfunction" is not much fun, though), neither did they help much. The response from the psychiatrist was to bring out the heavy guns and an antipsychotic drug was added to my drug diet to "augment" the antidepressant. Psychosis or schizophrenia was never part of my story, so this was an "off-label" use of this potent drug, a practice that has been increasing alarmingly in recent years. For the year I took this drug, I became a fat zombie couch potato, watching daytime TV, eating ice cream and doing little else. But even this dulling of my brain didn't work – my last major suicide attempt occurred while I was still on the heavy drug diet. The last and biggest gun in the armoury of psychiatry for "treatment-resistant" depression, and still seen as the gold standard, is electroconvulsive therapy (ECT). Fortunately I escaped the clutches of psychiatry before this was inflicted on me. With the current controversies around SSRI drugs in the United States, concerns are already being expressed that ECT, which psychiatrists admit to having no explanation for why "it seems to work", will be resorted to more frequently for depression.

My story has some parallels with that of William Styron's in *Darkness Visible* (which Bell refers to). The use of increasingly aggressive medical interventions is not uncommon, and it can have devastating consequences. The failure to look beyond the symptoms and the excessive reliance on medical interventions all rest on the *assumption* that depression is a medical illness. The reconceptualisation of depression as an illness rather than a symptom is part of the colonisation of what it is to be human by medicine and psychiatry, which Bell recognises when she admits that "allopathic rhetoric has colonised my thinking." She also cites a "rebel cry" from a psychiatrist who dared to challenge his colleagues that "mainstream psychiatry is now limited to a radical materialist ideology." This radical ideology is now the intellectual foundation of modern psychiatry which, supported by big pharma and extreme economic rationalism (see below), completes the conquest.

Depression is best understood as psychological *pain*. We do not think of physical pain as an illness but as an indication or symptom of some underlying physical illness or injury, which may require medical attention. A distinguished pioneer in the field of suicide prevention, Professor Edwin S. Shneidman, understood this when he coined the term *psychache* as the central feature of suicidal thinking and behaviour. Disenchanted with the DSM and its "specious accuracy built on a false epistemology", Shneidman defines psychache as psychological pain due to frustrated or thwarted psychological needs – the "specious accuracy" is the DSM's statistical clustering of symptoms, and the "false epistemology" the assumption that depression is a medical illness. Shneidman is now in his eighties and laments, as I do, the increasing medicalisation of human suffering. His notion of psychache, however, remains a much more useful starting point for understanding "depression" than the broken-brain, radical-materialist ideology of modern psychiatry.

In a similar way, antidepressants are best understood as psychological or emotional painkillers. If you break your leg, then it's a good idea to have some morphine. But it's a big mistake to think that the morphine will heal the broken bone. Taking drugs to ease extreme emotional pain can also serve a useful purpose, such as helping to create some time and space to think about maybe not killing yourself. I would argue, though, that if the anguish is severe enough to warrant potent drugs like antidepressants, then it is severe enough to warrant hospitalisation – but preferably the "benign detention" and "sequestration" that Bell refers to as the keys to William Styron's recovery from suicidal depression. Drugs can ease the pain while the real healing takes place. But, as with the broken leg, we don't simply take morphine forever and nothing else. The break in the bone has to be identified, reset and immobilised and other supports put in place while the healing occurs. Likewise with "depression". Except that under the broken-brain school of psychiatry, someone with a history like mine will likely be told, as I was, that I would need to take antidepressants for the rest of my life – and that no other "treatment" was relevant. Once more, this response to psychache rests entirely on the ideological assumption that depression is a medical illness, and specifically an illness of the brain.

Although I acknowledge a place for medications to ease extreme mental anguish, there are many complex questions about the suitability of the current

SSRI drugs for this purpose. Bell covers most of these but we can continue our analogy with morphine to summarise them. Morphine is a relatively "clean", benign, reliable and rapid-acting drug. Apart from the risk of addiction with long-term use, there are few risks if it is used in the correct way for pain relief. In contrast, modern SSRI emotional painkillers are decidedly peculiar. First, their efficacy is problematic – they seem to help some people but not others (and no one has an explanation for this). Next, they take at least a few weeks to "kick in", which can be a problem if suicide is a concern. Then they have a peculiar side-effect profile. With morphine, the main side effect is constipation and perhaps some nausea. With SSRIs probably the most common side effect, as mentioned, is "sexual dysfunction" (of varying kinds), but agitation, sleep disturbances (including nightmares) and problems with appetite are also quite common. We are also hearing now, as Bell reports, that these drugs can induce depression and suicidal feelings in some people, especially when first going on them, when the dose is changed or when coming off them. And although the popular myth is that these drugs are not addictive, we are also now learning of many who suffer quite extreme "discontinuation syndrome" symptoms, to use the psychobabble of big pharma and psychiatry. These are decidedly peculiar drugs, which is hardly surprising as they are complex, potent synthetic chemicals carefully designed to get past our protective "brain barrier" but which, unlike opiates, alcohol and other psycho-active drugs (or "intoxicants"), are totally foreign to our evolutionary, biological history. As Bell says, careful control, management and supervision of these drugs is essential – but it rarely occurs. Her plea that "you can't just give an adolescent a prescription and send them on their way" is not only the exception to current practice, it should also apply equally to adults.

Mention must also be made of another reconstruction of depression that works hand in hand with the medical reconceptualisation. In the January 2001 issue of the *Medical Journal of Australia*, Professor Gordon Parker, from the School of Psychiatry at the University of New South Wales, wrote:

> The number of people with depression is not growing substantially, despite historical formulations of depression as a response, a disorder, an illness and a disease. Its recent reformulation as a major economic cost due to its disabling effects, endorsed by the World Bank, Harvard University and the World Health Organisation, provided the spin, attracting public, media, health department and political attention.

The leading proponent in Australia of this economic rationalist "reformulation" – and of the political spin – is the beyondblue organisation chaired by former Victorian premier, Jeff Kennett. If you visit the beyondblue website you will find little to distinguish it from the depression pages on the websites of big pharma. The many controversies surrounding depression and its treatment, such as those raised by Gail Bell and others, are barely mentioned. In my first meeting with Professor Ian Hickie, the former CEO of and now consulting psychiatrist to beyondblue, some years ago, I argued that these controversies were a relevant and important part of the public debate on depression. His response was, "What controversies?" I have since learned many times that beyondblue does not welcome dissenting voices to its public relations spin. Given that it has received about $100 million of public funding (at last count) to sponsor a national "depression awareness" debate, this is tantamount to censorship in my view, censorship in the service of the "reformulation" that Professor Barker describes above.

The economic rationalist motivation of beyondblue is the growing realisation of the economic costs of depression and anxiety. Too many people are either unable or unwilling to work – taking too many "mental health sickies" – because of what should properly be called psychosocial distress. The World Bank, which is where the much-touted figure of 1-in-5 people suffering from depression comes from, expresses this in terms of the "global burden" of depression. In Australia, beyondblue is a major player in this disease-mongering that captures more and more people in the mental illness net.

In a special supplement to the July 2001 issue of the Medical Journal of Australia, beyondblue proposed a screening tool of twelve questions to assist doctors in the detection of mental illness. Space does not allow a full critique of all the flaws in this screening tool, but they can be illustrated by a simple example. One of the twelve questions the questionnaire asks is whether, "over the past few weeks" you have been "feeling constantly under strain?" According to this screening tool, known as SPHERE-12, if you answer this question with "most of the time", then you probably have a mental illness. The supplement is careful to say that the tool "is not a diagnostic system that will immediately lead to the delivery of specific treatments", but describes its purpose as being "to recognise a common mental disorder in a patient whose responses to the 12 items ... show sufficient symptoms to justify a diagnosis". Feeling constantly under strain most of the time over the past few weeks meets the SPHERE-12 criteria to justify a diagnosis. Many other very common life situations could also easily "justify a diagnosis", such as caring for young children, work stresses, being sacked from your job or having a boss who is a bully, to mention just a few. Oddly, when this tool later appeared on the *beyondblue* website, permitting us anonymously to screen ourselves, the threshold for risk of mental illness was very much higher than the advice given to doctors in the *MJA* supplement.

The extremely wide net cast by diagnostic tools such as SPHERE-12 is consistent with the wide net of the diagnostic criteria of the *DSM*. Few people, when evaluated against such criteria, would escape the label of a psychiatric diagnosis – I don't know anyone who does not qualify for at least one psychiatric diagnosis according to the criteria of the *DSM*. This is disease-mongering, the colonisation of the human psyche by medical ideology in partnership with the marketing of big pharma and the economic rationalism of organisations such as the World Bank and *beyondblue*. Or, as the title of the recent book by Ray Moynihan and Alan Cassels aptly puts it, this is *Selling Sickness: How Drug Companies Are Turning Us All into Patients*. To drug companies, I would add psychiatry and politicians.

The vast bulk of spending on mental health in Australia assumes the medical model of "mental illness". Governments and other policy-makers have bought the ideological myth of the medical, pharmaceutical and economic rationalist colonisation. Despite a clamour from mental health consumers, and also many non-clinical workers in mental health, for something more than the simplistic "diagnose and drug" approach of psychiatry, the insatiable appetite of medicine for expensive resources, combined with its political clout, means that few resources are available for non-medical responses to psychosocial distress. Follow the money and you will see the colonisation at work.

David Webb

Gail Bell

One of the principal aims of my essay was to call attention to the significant rise in antidepressant use in Australia in the past five years. The numbers alone ought to trip a warning siren. Twelve million antidepressant prescriptions dispensed through the National Health Scheme in 2004. Carve up the total any way you want, it's a lot of doses to swallow, a lot of computer key-strokes or pen scribbles by physician fingers, a lot of money passing from consumers to doctors, from consumers to pharmacists, from pharmacists to drug warehouses, and on down the line from the middlemen to the drug manufacturers. And the figure of twelve million doesn't include drug orders written for hospital in-patients, or capture the ones who got away – the patients who put their pieces of paper in a drawer instead of handing them to the pharmacist when doubts or economic factors or something they heard on television intervened after their trip to the doctor.

Having raised the red flag, I sought to humble myself before the mountains of information available on changing trends in the classification of depression and its treatment (principally antidepressant drug therapy), with an eye to finding a source for this eruption.In the wake of Prozac's fall from grace, and the increasing public demand for drug company accountability, an obvious starting point seemed to be big pharma. Indeed the working title of an early draft of the essay was Drug Companies and Depression. Drug company money washes in and out of this story, a bit like the tides one sees on parts of the Cornish coast; generously buoyant on the in-rush and heartlessly high-and-dry on the retreat. Drug company money keeps the prescription-writers afloat during their training by funding medical education, university departments, hospitals, research institutes and entrepreneurial chemical labs; and it maintains the comfort factor into the middle years with conferences near golf courses and five-star accommodation. As long as big pharma sees a return for its dollars, it will maintain the incoming tides. Following the money, as my correspondent David Webb recommends, leads the researcher to the multinationals' doors, but also to our own National Health Scheme which can't be overlooked as a contributor to the dominance of drug-based therapies for depression. In 2004 the NHS contributed $342 million in subsidies for antidepressant prescription costs.

My concerns were in place, however, long before I ever saw the figure of twelve million. Over the last ten years of a thirty-year watch at the dispensing coalface I've witnessed the increase in numbers first-hand. I saw Zoloft move from its alphabetical placement on the dispensary shelf into the frequent flyer division, at arm's reach for quick access and labelling. Only an automaton, or the truly disaffected, could ignore a phenomenon that involved large numbers of patients with complex symptoms being processed uniformly through a single portal.

But it is a distortion of the total picture to single out big pharma for exclusive attention. I made a decision early on to widen the goalposts. To quote myself: "I want to suggest that this impressive, noticeable increase in antidepressant usage in Australia today has come about through the co-operation of three large but inherently unequal groups: the multinational drug companies; the physicians who write prescriptions; and the public who turn to medicine for answers."

Three groups, not one. And more complexity, not less. Guy Rundle points out, very eloquently, that "a whole level of social life and social process" was not taken into account in my essay as it attempted to diagnose the causes of increased reliance on drugs to treat depression. I couldn't agree more, and I was careful to note in the essay's sources (#6) the lines of enquiry I considered to be outside the scope of my brief. The patient/drug interface is, I believe, an under-represented source of empirical evidence. Social scientists are welcome to interpret the significance of these findings for the wider culture, as seen from this relatively unfamiliar vantage point.

Professor Gordon Parker, psychiatrist and head of The Black Dog Institute, has provided a lucid history lesson in his response. He reminds us that modern medicine has been devising typologies aimed at better classification of depression since the 1950s, acknowledges the emergence of a "procrustean model" where the patient is in effect stretched to meet the length of the bed, and argues for a "horse for courses" model; all of which, if I read my own work correctly, were covered in the essay. This concordance, however, breaks down dramatically when Professor Parker expresses his concerns. I am accused of taking a "pull up your socks", ad hominem attitude towards those with significant mood disorders. Worse, my words are "misanthropic, trivialising and belittling". His argument takes the following surreal path: I tried an antidepressant and it didn't work for me, therefore I have channelled my inner bitterness and disappointment into a hatchet job on those whose lives have been changed for the better by SSRIs. Paternalistic huff aside, this is an odd and worrying response from a medical man whose reputation is built on astute judgments. My own position, clearly stated from the outset, is pro-patient. They (we) must never be underestimated. Gone are the days of the divine physician and the silent apothecary. Questions must be asked up and down the line; and answers, where possible, must be given. If we are to maintain our relevance against the loquacious, ever-available internet search engines, we must offer what a machine cannot: wisdom and compassion and a degree of humility.

With regard to two worrying expressions, "The Worried Well" and "misery chic", I make the following remarks. For Professor Parker's sake I regret that "misery chic" became detached from its qualifying clause in successive drafts of the essay. It belongs to the vocabulary of the Prozac phenomenon of the '90s and comes from the book Prozac Nation. My correspondent "Angie" to whom the postcard section was addressed was familiar with its import and needed no amplification, but for the benefit of readers who may have felt slightly jolted by its impact, I offer the following. The term was invented and first used in New York. As the uptake of Prozac escalated beyond all projections in the United States, "depression" acquired fad status, and from "fad" came "chic".

The prominence of "The Worried Well" seems to have impeded Elizabeth A. Wilson's ability to read beyond the title of the essay. And this leads me to a suggestion for the regulators whose demanding task it is to apply labels when describing the diagnosis and treatment of depression. Abandon the words "mild" "moderate" and "severe". Abandon the procrustean model of fitting the patient to the disease (as described by Professor Parker). Apply the clinical sophistication that modern training is supposed to confer on our physicians and consider each person on his or her own merits. As one psychiatrist recently told me, "severe" depression should mean "the depression I'm seeing in this patient is as bad as it gets for him or her". Treat accordingly. Drugs perhaps. Lifestyle changes. Counselling.

I'm writing this response a week after a visit with Angie, whose story featured in my essay. She is back from four months in New York and has had time to absorb the personal implications of having a literary snapshot of controversial aspects of her life circulated widely in print. Even under a disguised name and hidden inside a trench coat of deliberately misleading clues, she has been recognised by her nearest and dearest, and quizzed. I engineered this follow-up meeting because I felt a duty of care towards Angie. It is one thing to grant an author permission to use quotes and observations; it is often quite another to read what an author makes of intimate revelations. The one subject we didn't discuss was Zoloft, the focal point of our first and subsequent encounters. Why? Because, in essence, it's none of my business whether she maintains, escalates, tapers or even ceases her doses altogether. Our relationship mirrors, in many respects, the relationships I form with patients in the pharmacy. It is respectful, episodic; noses are not poked in where they are not wanted. I chose Angie's story from hundreds, perhaps thousands, of stories I've heard in a long career dispensing mood-altering drugs because she was articulate, candid and confident in narrating her experience of depressive episodes; and because she exemplified the "just dose me up" class of patients, a group who interest me personally. Those who seek (rightly) to destigmatise depression must be discouraged from dumbing down the really useful message about depression: that it is complex, that one person's dark night of the soul is not the same as the next person's, that what works for one does not necessarily work for all.

From the viewpoint of someone who works in the drug delivery system (a coalface, I might argue, that is deeper in the mineshaft than the university library shelf), it is blindingly obvious that antidepressants are over-used. But that is not to say that antidepressants represent the wrong choice for the treatment of depression, merely that at this time, in this country, the drug option is over-represented and some attempts to restore balance are called for.

Gail Bell

Moira Rayner

Children begin by loving their parents; after a time they judge them;
rarely, if ever, do they forgive them.

—Oscar Wilde

Wilde's great private grief was over losing all contact with his sons because he
was a homosexual, not because he was a bad father. Nobody consulted the boys
because the law, judges and society of the day assumed a homosexual, and thus
a criminal, could not be a "good" father, and that cutting all contact with a bad
parent[1] was in a child's best interests.

We have made progress since the nineteenth century. Until 1975, husbands
still had automatic sole custody of their children, which police would enforce
until a court made a contrary order, but common-law courts and Australia's *Mat-
rimonial Causes Act* required custody and access disputes to be decided on the basis
of the paramountcy of the child's best interests. But in 1992 High Court Justice
Brennan pointed out, in Marion's case,[2] that a best interests approach depends
on the value system of the decision-maker. Without any rule or guideline, it
simply creates an unexaminable discretion in the repository of the power.

That case was about the Family Court's power to authorise a non-therapeutic
hysterectomy of an intellectually disabled girl. Brennan J. argued that the proper
starting point was not the value judgment about the child's best interests, but
the child's human rights; and that even an intellectually disabled child had the
right to be consulted about a decision that would lead to such an intrusion on
her body.

His was a still, small voice. The UN Convention on the Rights of the Child
was not then and is not today incorporated in Australian law. Best interests, and
judges' values, rule.

There are plenty of real issues about the way both the law and the courts deal with decisions affecting children. Unfortunately, John Hirst's essay avoids virtually all of them.

Courts are a crude tool for cutting down the wreckage of intimate relationships. Of course, mediated disputes work out better, because the parties themselves decide what is "good enough" and can live with the compromise, especially if children are involved. Most arguments end there. The federal government's foreshadowed legal presumption of "equal responsibility" for parental child-care decisions after separation will not make courts any more suitable for recreating happy families or righting wrongs in the fractious 5 per cent of family law disputes that they have to decide.

What is lacking in John Hirst's essay and in family law policy-making is respect for the child's point of view. His case studies are about unjustly treated children, as told by fathers in need of vindication. Unfair outcomes are attributed to bias, to mother-favouring courts and judges tainted by feminism. Children are assumed to be inanimate non-participants, or weapons, in their parents' family wars. There is no grasp of the philosophical effect of Australia's ratification of the UN Convention on the Rights of the Child in 1990, which committed our government to respect all children's rights – to a family environment of love and understanding in which their full potential is most likely to be achieved; to parental guidance; to protection from exploitation, neglect and cruelty; and to express a view and have it taken seriously in justly made decisions affecting them.

Hirst's is a trumpet blast against a monstrous regiment of women[3] and what he sees as their illegitimate exploitation of family power. Yet for every father's grievance, there is a mother's, too. Not one of the women's stories, which I know John Hirst was told in his research for this essay, is even mentioned in it. On the one hand, Hirst criticises the ALP for aligning its policy with feminists' causes, yet on the other he has nothing to say about conservatives riding the wave of men's anger, fuelled by talkback radio or conservative think-tanks from which commentators argue for the return of fault-based divorce and against the human rights of children.

Hirst's essay recites men's grievances. The real defects of family law lie far deeper. Litigation outcomes are poor because the hardest cases go to trial and Solomon does not sit in those courts: be thankful. Judges know little about child development and the effects of abuse, but we haven't yet fully explored how they could learn from those disciplines, and experts, that do. Courts don't readily adapt their adult-oriented processes so that children can participate in them: until they can hear what children say with or without words, they will make terrible errors. Lawyers aren't trained to listen to children or assess their maturity to give instructions, yet when they become judges they must decide whether children sufficiently understand "the truth" to give evidence, or right and wrong, to assume criminal responsibility.

The Family Court was never meant to be adversarial, as Hirst assumes when, because of the injustice to fathers wrongly accused of sexual offences against their children, he argues that the courts should abandon the "unacceptable risk" test for deciding disputed child sex abuse allegations. The privacy of the family, the presumption of innocence and the silence of the child make such claims impossible to prove or disprove. No court anywhere has the power to make a binding declaration that a man is innocent or "clear his name", as Hirst wishes the Family Court to do.

Terrible damage is done to children's relationships because family law litigation takes too long. Why, given the pain and distress it causes, doesn't Hirst have anything to say about the federal government's decision to establish a separate Federal Magistrates Court rather than reform the Family Court and include magistrates within it? Why does he have nothing sensible to say about the complex and fractured state of children's court/child protection legislation, reporting systems and variations in expert evidence and standards of proof, which are major contributors to some of the injustices he has documented? These are far more important than the perceived bias or hauteur of a particular court or chief justice.

John Hirst presents his case as champion of fathers engaged in adversarial, parent-to-parent, combat. How else can he argue that the punishment for "contempt" by mothers who do not comply with contact orders should not be moderated by its effect on the best interests of a child in their care? He supports mediation, but overlooks or perhaps does not know of the continuing practice of excluding children from it – an old practice and a poor one. Twenty years ago on the instructions of a fourteen-year-old girl who wanted the Family Court of Western Australia to sort out her parents' ongoing war over "access", which they wouldn't sort out, I made a written application for definition of access. Both (surprised and defensive) parents turned up; the judge referred the parties for immediate counselling; but when I went up to the waiting room a couple of hours later my client was sitting alone while Mum and Dad argued about their marriage with a counsellor. I raised merry hell, she got into the room, the whole thing got sorted, but attitudes have not changed. And there's another remarkable lack: John Hirst says nothing at all about the role of children's representatives. The presence of a trained, competent child representative helps to shift parents' focus away from their own wounds and onto their child as a person, not a forensic object.

John Hirst and I agree on some things. Courts should be a last resort for sorting out the children's needs, for example, though in my experience most parents won't negotiate, except at a courtroom door. We can agree that dads are as important as mums and ought to be actively involved in parenting and give up too easily — I have heard far too many fathers explain their non-involvement by their need to "walk away" from personal pain; I have also seen plenty, too, who were willing to sacrifice their own immediate happiness to care for their children's.

If our family law is to be changed, I would like to see the rights of children take their proper place. Access should be an enforceable right of a child, with some sanction on a parent who hurts a child by making arrangements to, for example, take a child out or attend a school function, and does not turn up. I fail to comprehend the ethics of John Hirst's argument that a father who does not see his children should not have to maintain them: how long, after all, does a child maintenance obligation persist? Why should a choice to start a second family see the first go without? I had a client, once, whose husband left her with seven children, whom she could not feed and clothe, though she made the bread, dressed them in cast-offs and grew their vegetables, because he had remarried and arranged his finances to avoid paying child support. He didn't bother visiting. I remember how readily, twenty-five years ago, country magistrates suspended and expunged arrears of child maintenance owed by temporarily unemployed fathers and how hard it was for mothers to afford fresh maintenance applications when they got new jobs. I used to see hungry kids in shabby flats whose sleek, gift-bearing access visitors gave them a taste of a different life, then fled. It was the injustices of the law on children that made me focus on their human rights.

John Hirst's essay was a disappointment. His arguments connect with the feudal history of custody rules and the possessory rights of fathers, not the modern view that children have human rights, and adults an enforceable responsibility to subordinate their own preferences to these rights. There is no appreciation of the traditional, political and resource obstacles to the Family Court's achievement of its purpose. Its argument is predicated on win/lose, competition and blame. Men may well be angry about the effect that the social changes of the last forty years have had on them. We ought to admit that they had some unintended consequences, but they cannot be undone. Fault-based divorce laws were discriminatory and ended marriages without dignity and in unfairness: a major justification for Murphy's law[4] was to stop jailing men who did not pay maintenance. Of course, women should be entitled to choose whether to have children and to work, but there is nothing wrong with admitting that this sometimes makes it hard on children, too. So do fathers' decisions to set up second families while the first still need them.

While acknowledging the anguish behind dads' anger we must do something about the continuing lack of respect for children's rights. John Hirst's argument drowns out the voices of children.

Moira Rayner

1   In those days the "unfit" parent was usually proven to be an adulterous mother, not a heterosexually straying husband who automatically had the sole custody of the children of the marriage.
2   *Marion's Case.* 1992 175 CLR 218
3   Sottish theological iconoclast John Knox issued a pamphlet against Mary, Queen of Scots under a similar title. I do not accuse John Hirst of misogyny or of religious, at least, fundamentalism.
4   Lionel Murphy was the federal ALP Attorney General who introduced the *Family Law Act 1975*.

Bruce Hawthorne

John Hirst raises many salient issues. However, in his attempt to champion the cause of many deeply aggrieved non-resident fathers, it is a pity that he allows his acrimony to infiltrate his essay and sometimes to cloud his judgment. His understanding of how the family law system operates is surprisingly accurate for someone who admits to having played only a minor role in one of its many dramas. He has highlighted some of the legal strategies employed to gain advantage in parenting disputes before the Court, and the injustices that sometimes result. He has, however, fallen into the trap of arguing from the particular to the general in interpreting some individuals' experiences of the system as indicative of the Court's policies and procedures. It is not standard procedure for parents to surrender contact with children in order to receive news of them. It is highly unlikely that most officers of the Court take an Apprehended Violence Order as prima facie evidence that violence has occurred between the parties. They recognise that many Apprehended Violence Orders around the time of separation are about safeguarding boundaries that one or other party is unwilling to respect.

In the thirty years since the establishment of the Family Court, growing numbers of fathers have become more involved in their children's lives and have assumed greater responsibility for them, sometimes by choice and sometimes because of mothers' greatly increased participation in paid employment. As intact family life has changed, pressure has grown for changes to separated family life. The current political influence exercised by non-resident fathers, whose frustration and pain Hirst has clearly identified, is an attempt to convince both legislators and policy-makers of the need for that change.

Hirst bravely ventures into a minefield when he challenges the weight given by the legislation and the Court to the best interests of children after parents separate. In 1975, when the *Family Law Act* was introduced, there were very real fears that no-fault divorce would lead to widespread abandoning of marital commitments and to increasing numbers of children becoming the "innocent victims" of divorce. It was socially imperative for legislation and practice to protect children, even though there was then very little quality research into the impact of divorce. Now, however, children of separated parents are no longer the social oddity they may have been thirty years ago. Many children of divorced parents score as well as children in intact families on measures of adjustment. Research has also shown children usually benefit from both parents in their lives, provided they do not become ensnared in ongoing inter-parental conflict.

Family law rhetoric and practice are very much about the best interests and rights of children, and the responsibilities rather than the rights of parents. Hirst cites incidents where seemingly innocent non-resident fathers have been denied contact or involvement with children in the belief that such contact is not in children's best interests. While rejecting his somewhat patronising description of the Court as "pious", I suggest that both the legislation and jurisprudence appear precious at times. They seek to provide children in separated families with the sort of privileged position that most children in intact families do not enjoy. Families generally do not always function on the principle of children's best interests. What frequently happens in a healthy family life is that parents do not live for their children but seek to strike a reasonable balance between the rights, needs and interests of all family members. How many get the balance right is a matter of conjecture. Families in which children's interests always prevail do not seem any healthier than those in which they are consistently swamped by those of parents. Competing interests are often evident, for example, when parents relocate for employment or lifestyle reasons. Although the relocation usually results in children experiencing short-term deprivation and pain, it may be to their long-term benefit. Nevertheless, parents' claims that they are relocating because their children's interests are paramount still deserve to be met with scepticism.

The reluctance to recognise parents' rights along with their responsibilities is surprising. Making children's best interests the paramount consideration in resolving disputes seems to distance the family law system from what commonly happens in intact family life. It is little wonder that many non-resident fathers complain that the system is gender-biased, accusing it of marginalising them within the family, denying their rights and failing to enforce contact orders contravened by resident mothers. It is unclear, though, whether the bias is gender-based or the product of the sole-residence arrangement.

Hirst cites cases to do with children's names and family relocation to demonstrate the almost exclusive authority that resident parents (the vast majority of whom are mothers) enjoy. The 1995 *Family Law Reform Act* has effectively restricted the resident parent's right to relocate with children, but there remains a very telling example of this authority. Court orders commonly direct resident parents to authorise schools to communicate details of children's academic progress to non-resident parents and to inform them of significant school events. How resident parents ever gained the authority to prevent that flow of information remains unclear. Just as puzzling is the reason why schools, as a matter of policy, do not automatically include both separated parents in the information loop in the absence of any court order to the contrary.

This example shows that systemic forces impede non-resident parents from having substantial involvement in children's lives and restrict their opportunity to exercise parental authority. The irony of it all is that the authority bestowed on resident parents was largely an attempt to protect children from becoming ensnared in potentially harmful, ongoing inter-parental conflict. Yet some research reports that a sense of being unable to exercise parental authority is strongly associated with ongoing hostility between parents. The following comment by a non-resident father captures the ambiguity that many men encounter in their post-separation fathering:

> I grew up as a young man when society was actively encouraging men to be involved in their families. Attend the birth, go to school meetings, read to your child, etc, etc. Quality time was the mantra. And many of us took this on, albeit imperfectly in many cases; after all, where was our role model? Our fathers did not do it. But then the relationship breaks up and then you are the disposable parent … can it be a surprise that some men are pushed to doing irrational things? I think not.

Hirst accurately recognises that difficult families requiring a judicial decision have become the template for other separating families. Many non-resident fathers, often on solicitors' advice, simply do not apply to the Court for substantial involvement with children. They rather settle for a level of contact that they would expect to receive should they contest the matter in court. (However, since the *Reform Act*, court orders now more often provide for non-resident parents to have contact with children during the week as well as on alternate weekends, and to be responsible for day-to-day decisions when the children are in their care.) Some resident mothers, too, use the "court standard" of contact on alternate weekends and for half the school holidays as the criterion by which they measure their goodwill or generosity in offering contact to non-resident fathers.

For this reason, the adoption of shared residence for children as a rebuttable presumption may have a profound effect by shifting the implied template for all separating parents. It will very likely influence attitudes. Parents may well invest more energy and time in trying to salvage their relationship when faced with the child-support implications of shared residence and the substantial separation from children that it implies. Having decided to separate, they may be willing to come to negotiations about their new family arrangement on a more equal footing. Presently, because of the general expectation that children will live with mothers after separation, many fathers have no input into decisions about residence and contact, and perceive that their involvement with children and parental authority depends entirely on mothers' goodwill.

Not all separated fathers want a shared-residence arrangement. As Hirst states, the call for joint custody is partly symbolic, reflecting many non-resident fathers' desire for greater involvement in children's lives and the chance to exercise parental authority. Certainly, those for whom fatherhood is of little significance are unlikely to want to assume responsibility for children for substantial periods of time. For some, work demands and geographical distance render shared residence an impracticable arrangement. For some, family violence, substance abuse, psychiatric disturbance and limited parenting skills rule it out as a viable option. For others, though, shared residence, or at least the opportunity to exercise significant parental authority within the family is what they want, what they consider they have a right to, and what they are convinced will benefit their children.

Bruce Hawthorne

Lawrie Moloney

All large organisations falter. The question is why, how often and with what consequences. Alexander Downer recently admitted to Kerry O'Brien that the Passport Office loses about 2000 new passports each year. He claims it issues about a million per annum. Is that an acceptable ratio? Is there a systemic problem? What if a few found their way to "terrorists"? Some years ago, an incorrect computer entry led an Air New Zealand plane to fly directly into Mt Erebus. Was it one mistake? Was it one of many mistakes ignored or undetected until then? Whatever the answer, the consequences were disastrous.

Like many before him, John Hirst's excursion into family law in Australia began with a personal experience of injustice – an initial misjudgment by the Court, but one that was compounded by neglect. Hirst was recruited into co-operating with a Family Court order to supervise a young separated man accused of being a danger to his family, while he spent time with his children. What he experienced was a capable loving father doing all the things a normal competent parent would do. Why did the Court require that he be "supervised"? Thus began Hirst's emotive, astute, wide-ranging but somewhat patchy inquiry into the Family Court.

The title of Hirst's essay, "Kangaroo Court", leaves us in no doubt about where this inquiry took him. A core determination is to be found in one of his concluding statements: "The Family Court is a monstrosity, a court of law that cannot by its no-fault charter be a court of justice."

Hirst builds towards this conclusion through a mix of personal criticism, especially of former Chief Justice Nicholson, several case studies that end up dishing out bad deals to men, selected statements from judgments, and an interesting though incomplete socio-legal analysis of our profound ambivalence about some of the consequences of "no-fault divorce". Some of his calls for "fundamental change" are spot-on. Some are a little underdeveloped. One or two are, I believe, misinformed.

The criticism of Alistair Nicholson is not without merit. There is no doubt that he acted at times like the doctor who complained that all he saw every day were sick people. Male litigants were a frequent target. Nicholson was publicly sceptical of those aspects of the mid-'90s *Family Law Reform Act* that were meant to encourage a greater sense of shared parenting after separation and divorce. In 2000 he strongly endorsed a Court-sponsored research report which concluded (with virtually no evidence to support the finding) that the main reason men were applying for increased parenting time was to continue to exercise control over their former partners. He suggested that the report demonstrated the *Reform Act* had fundamentally failed.

It is perhaps significant that around this time the Court had also begun to declare that its core mission was to focus on cases of violence and abuse. The problem was that many "ordinary" cases seemed to become caught up in the same web of expectations. Hirst's case studies reflect errors and neglect, but also a systemic problem that the Court has struggled to solve. Allegations of violence or child abuse (usually made by women against men) need to be taken seriously. Judges and magistrates usually have insufficient evidence to determine the truth of the matter at an interim hearing stage. They try to balance the need to protect and the right of children in normal circumstances to continue a relationship with their father.[1] Inevitably they don't always get this balance right.

Hirst's more telling point, however, relates to consequences and follow-up. There is little doubt that the Court has struggled to investigate allegations in an adequate and timely way, especially after interim decisions have been made. There also seems to be a reluctance to attach consequences to allegations that are made with malicious intent.

Hirst sees the nature of that struggle as primarily ideological. I'm inclined to agree. Although inadequate investigation and attention to false allegations in some ways also reflect resource problems, one cannot credibly sustain a resource defence in the face of the addition of the Federal Magistrates Court and the fact that the problem has existed for so long. A child of the chaos that surrounded the 1975 double dissolution, the Family Court was significantly under-resourced from the outset. But almost thirty years on, the more important question is where to place the resources that currently exist.

Hirst describes one attempt the Family Court made to fast-track alleged abuse cases. He correctly notes that, though methodologically flawed, the Magellan Project engaged with some critical issues to do with identification, case management and the old chestnut of Commonwealth/State rivalry and buck-passing. Interestingly, Magellan's most important legacy to date has been the more comprehensive and carefully evaluated Columbus Project that it helped spawn in the Family Court of Western Australia. The project is described elsewhere.[2] Though it is still early days, it is clear that some of the problems that beset the Court in the other states would be far less likely to occur if a model like this were to be adopted

Late in the essay, Hirst touches on some of the profound issues that family law has to tackle. Before he arrives at this analysis, however, his dominant narrative describes fathers whose alleged violence is assumed to be true from the outset, whose capacity to nurture their children is greeted with scepticism but who nevertheless should be content to pay significant amounts of child support regardless of how much or how little their relationship with their children is supported by the Court or by the other parent.

I too have written on these issues. I have great sympathy for the many men I see who have wanted to do "the right thing" for their families and who are frequently shattered when a partner announces (twice as likely to be the case as the other way around) that she wants out because he has failed. Frequently these men are told they have misunderstood the nature of this "right thing". In addition, their commitment to supporting their families financially may have contributed to estrangement from their partners and possibly their children. "Now all of a sudden", I have heard some of those partners complain, "you want to be father of the year."

I also have great sympathy for single mothers living near or below the poverty line who have either been abandoned by the father of the children or who, perhaps for reasons like those above, cannot see the relevance of input from him and now simply wish him to go away. These are human tragedies that are set against a background of complex and contradictory expectations embedded in our culture. The expectations are both reflected and interpreted within a piece of legislation that operates at its heart through adversarial processes.

Hirst recognises that no analysis of family law can avoid commentary on the adversary system. It begins with the first solicitor's letter to "the other party", frequently sprinkled with allegations and ambit claims, and generally goes downhill from there. It is an extraordinarily destructive system when applied to disputes between two individuals who once loved each other and who need to work out how to continue to be good parents. The fact that it is used and modified in good faith by many caring family lawyers does not justify its continuation.

Yuri Joakamidis's "maximising parenting time" recommendation is where the essay formally ends. I am aware of no evidence to support the claim upon which this rests. Hirst appears to endorse Joakamidis's claim that, "It is the parent, woman or man, who thinks they will control the children who usually breaks up a marriage." Hirst's further claim that a maximising of time presumption could drive the divorce rate down is a bold one indeed. And the additional assertion, that this would in turn protect the best interests of children, suggests an inadequate understanding of what impacts most on a child – not divorce or separation itself, but ongoing unresolved conflict. Divorce is not an ideal outcome for children, but they can cope if (preferably both) parents remain attuned to their needs. On the other hand entrenched parental conflict, whether inside or outside a marriage, is frightening for children. How can they feel safe when the parents on whom they rely appear to not be in charge of themselves?

Hirst's desire to prescribe outcomes for parenting disputes in advance has echoes of the very "totalitarian impulse" he sees in the Court in another context. But the biggest issue I have with both the presumption of maximum time and the "hit the backsliders hard" aspect of Hirst's analysis is respect for the agency of the children themselves. Hirst sees the latitude granted to decision-makers in interpreting the best interests of the child as a major part of the problem. Applied to non-adversarial processes, which Hirst advocates for all Family Court proceedings, I see it as part of the solution.

There is a large range of issues around the "best interests" question, discussion of which would fill a modest-sized bookshelf. Hirst is either unaware of this or chooses not to go there. But the fact is that most formal reviews of the decision-making principles that should be applied in family law, whether informed by feminist principles or not, return to individualised interpretations of the best interests of the child as the best guiding principle.

They return there for a variety of reasons, but one of the most basic is that children should not be commodified by deciding in advance where their interests lie. Clients in the Children in Focus[3] program, which I co-direct with a colleague, Jenn McIntosh, teach us over and over again that each child has a unique set of responses to parental separation. I understand John Hirst's struggle to accept that if we do not apply a formula, albeit even a rebuttable one, our system is saying to separating couples, "You can do this! Suspend personal bitterness 'for the sake of the children' and work together as parents if not as partners." All I can offer in such a brief response is that there is a variety of ways that parents can be assisted to achieve such a goal and the results are frequently moving and startling. And I am enough of an optimist to believe that judges too can be taught these skills and learn to apply them if they are prepared to rise to the challenge of conducting non-adversarial proceedings.

Kangaroo court? In one research project I undertook, I looked carefully at the thinking behind parenting judgments in the Family Court. I found convincing evidence that men tended to be taken insufficiently seriously as nurturing parents. And women who did not conform to maternal stereotypes could also be harshly criticised. Then I looked at some of David de Vaus's work and found that these judgments were not too far removed from public sentiments. Tricky! I didn't look at alleged violence and abuse cases. Had I done so, I have little doubt the picture would have been even more complex.

Does the Court bungle a greater percentage of cases than the Passport Office? Probably! For one thing, separating families are infinitely more difficult to deal with than passports. Are most of its customers very unhappy with the service? Probably not! Do adversarial processes deal adequately with complex human situations? Very rarely. Are there serious consequences attached to leaving violence allegations in limbo, or failing to act on malicious allegations? Almost always!

A final comment. Hirst's hard-line tactics for dealing with backsliders includes a recommendation that obstruction of parenting opportunities should be responded to by a withdrawal of maintenance. The child-support formula can be harsh and needs revision. But withdrawal is not the answer. Although Hirst's recommendation has superficial appeal, it is highly adult-oriented and again places children at risk. The risk is only partially financial. As Hirst notes, the deficit may indeed be topped-up through increased supporting parent payments. But talk to a young adult who has learned that his or her father gave up on offering financial support – hardly the stuff to promote self-esteem or to encourage a relationship, even in those more extreme cases in which the relationship may only flourish in later life.

Lawrie Moloney

1   Hirst would put it as the right of the father to see his child.
2   Hirst notes some of unique features of the Family Court of Western Australia which, it might be argued, make it especially suited to implementing this more tightly managed approach. The Columbus Project is described on the Court's website. Its ongoing development and outcomes can also be followed in an article in *Family Matters* and in several articles in the *Journal of Family Studies*.
3   See www.childreninfocus.org

**Gail Bell** was educated in pharmacy and education at the University of Sydney and has worked as a pharmacist, drug educator, chemistry teacher, literacy tutor and occasional journalist. Her first book, *The Poison Principle*, won the NSW Premier's Prize for Non-Fiction in 2002. Her second book, *SHOT: A Personal Response to Guns and Trauma*, was released to critical acclaim in November 2003 and short-listed for the Nita B. Kibble Award.

**Judith Brett** is the author of *Robert Menzies' Forgotten People* and, most recently, *Australian Liberals and the Moral Middle Class: From Alfred Deakin to John Howard*. She has been a regular columnist for the *Age* and an editor of *Meanjin*. She is Professor of Politics at La Trobe University.

**Bruce Hawthorne** has worked for fourteen years as a counsellor in the Family Court. He recently completed a PhD on Australian non-resident fathers and the factors that influence their engagement with their children.

**Lawrie Moloney** is an associate professor in the School of Public Health at La Trobe University. He edits the *Journal of Family Studies*.

**Gordon Parker** is Scientia Professor of Psychiatry at the University of New South Wales and executive director of the Black Dog Institute, Sydney.

**Moira Rayner** is special counsel to the Council for Equal Opportunity in Employment Limited, a lawyer and a writer. She helped establish and chaired the Board of the National Children's and Youth Law Centre from 1993 and was director of the Office of the Children's Rights Commissioner for London in 2000. She is the author of *Rooting Democracy* and co-author, with Joan Kirner, of *The Woman's Power Handbook*.

**Guy Rundle** is an executive producer of ABC Arts. For many years he was the co-editor of *Arena* magazine. He is also the writer of political satires performed by Max Gillies and of *Quarterly Essay 3, The Opportunist: John Howard and the Triumph of Reaction*, published in 2001.

**David Webb** is about to complete a PhD at Victoria University on the lived experience of feeling suicidal. He is also the chairperson of the Victorian Mental Illness Awareness Council.

**Elizabeth A. Wilson** is a psychologist and an ARC Fellow in the Research Institute for Humanities and Social Science at the University of Sydney. She is the author of *Psychosomatic: Feminism and the Neurological Body*.